On My Honor

Real Life Lessons from
America's First Girl Scout

SHANNON HENRY KLEIBER

 sourcebooks

Published by Sourcebooks, Inc.
P.O. Box 4410, Naperville, Illinois 60567-4410
(630) 961-3900
Fax: (630) 961-2168
www.sourcebooks.com

Library of Congress Cataloging-in-Publication Data

Kleiber, Shannon Henry.
On my honor : real life lessons from America's first Girl Scout/Shannon Henry Kleiber.
Includes bibliographical references.
1. Girl Scouts of the United States of America. 2. Girl Scouts—United States. 3. Low,
Juliette Gordon, 1860–1927. I. Title.
HS3359.K56 2012
369.463092—dc23

2011047805

Printed and bound in the United States of America.
VP 10 9 8 7 6 5 4 3 2

For my daughters
Eve and Julia

ALSO BY SHANNON HENRY KLEIBER

The Dinner Club: How the Masters of
the Internet Universe Rode the Rise and Fall
of the Greatest Boom in History

"Have you ever stopped to think that your most constant companion throughout life will be yourself? You will always have this body, this mind, and this spirit that you call 'I,' but this body, this mind, and this spirit are constantly growing and changing, and it is quite possible for the owner to direct this growth and change. In order to live well, in order to possess the joy of life, and to be helpful to others, a Scout needs to apply her motto 'Be Prepared' to herself. Strength and beauty should be hers in body, mind, and spirit."

—From *How Girls Can Help Their Country*, adapted from Agnes Baden-Powell and Sir Robert Baden-Powell's Handbook (1916)

THE GIRL SCOUT PROMISE

On my honor, I will try:
To serve God and my country,
To help people at all times,
and to live by the Girl Scout Law.

THE GIRL SCOUT LAW

I will do my best to be
honest and fair,
friendly and helpful,
considerate and caring,
courageous and strong, and
responsible for what I say and do,
and to
respect myself and others,
respect authority,
use resources wisely,
make the world a better place, and
be a sister to every Girl Scout.

THE GIRL SCOUT MOTTO

Be Prepared

THE GIRL SCOUT SLOGAN

Do a Good Turn Daily

contents

introduction

itting in a close circle, the girls in the group buzz about being invited to the dance, a fight with a friend, schoolwork due the next day. It could be a scene from any high school, middle school, or even elementary school in the United States today. But I like to imagine it might just as easily be something like a moment at one of the first meetings of the Girl Scouts of the USA. The group, then called Girl Guides, started meeting one hundred years ago, with its leaders encouraging girls to become leaders of the future.

It was then that Juliette Gordon Low, affectionately known to everyone as Daisy, founded the Girl Scouts as a group to strengthen girls' characters through skill-building and learning individual responsibility. The Girl Scouts of today, like those of a century ago, thrive on friendships formed within the group and take what they have learned into adulthood. The story of Daisy is that of every American woman: that of finding herself. But it is also the tale of the woman who has influenced millions, who gave girls a voice even before they had a vote, or before they were likely to compete in a professional sport, run a company, or hold a patent.

Politicians, first ladies, journalists, and actresses are just a handful among the more than fifty million women who were once Girl Scouts. Girl Scouts are currently running our country: about half of the women now in Congress were once Girl Scouts. There are Girl Scouts in all fifty states, and of course, even famous former Girl Scouts, including Lucille Ball, Dorothy Hamill, and Katie Couric. Something every woman has in common as she is trying to find her place in the world is that she was, once, a girl. What happened or didn't happen to her then doesn't force any absolute outcomes, but it shapes in little and big ways the person she becomes. Daisy's character and how she formed the Girl Scouts continues to influence generations. To me, Daisy was a feminist, an environmentalist, and a self-help author (through her contributions in guidebooks), before anyone used those terms. She was forward-thinking not only in her early promotion of women's leadership, but also in the value she placed on service to others, and inclusivity for girls of diverse religions, races, and economic classes. As fellow Girl Scout leaders and former Girl Scouts know, what she founded defies any sort of simple categorization. Yet we still feel the power in the work she did all those years ago.

From my first days as a Girl Scout troop leader, I was struck by how relevant Daisy's advice still is for us today. So many of the things I want for my kids—spending more time outdoors, knowing where their food comes from, finding work they love, being a good friend—were all encouraged by Daisy and have become part of what Girl Scouts talk about and strive toward, together. I've also realized this is a particularly crucial moment to understand these lessons, as we are in many ways becoming overdependent on technology, less aware of the natural world around us, and most importantly, less connected to each other. In these times of cyber-bullying and social networking, we need to remember to make time to truly connect, and this is especially true of Girl Scout age girls, five- to seventeen-year-olds. We need to talk face to face with young girls, take walks together, and eat meals with each other. Developing real relationships is one of the true tenets of Girl Scouting, and one that guards against children falling through the cracks and feeling alone. When this understanding of human connection starts at an early age, it becomes part of a girl's internal fabric and helps her navigate the years ahead. I believe and have seen in my own troop that The Girl Scout uses her own intuition and knowledge to solve problems, developing a personal life compass. But at the same time, when a difficulty or roadblock comes up, she is less likely to feel alone, and will instead to look to her friends, including her sisters, to help her through the tough times. As Girl Scouts celebrates in 2012 its founding one hundred years ago by Daisy, the simple but profound encouragement of women seems more germane to our time than ever. It is what we need now, not just for the 3.2 million active members of Girl Scouts, but for our entire society.

Every intertwined aspect of Girl Scouting works to develop "courage, confidence, and character in young women." It happens not by lecturing the girls, but by guiding them to learn and accomplish things for themselves, to become, as many Girl Scouts call themselves, "Greenbloods." Juliette Gordon Low was much more than the namesake founder of the organization. Her personality, her way of looking at the world, and her irrepressible *joie de vivre* can be seen and felt in generation after generation of Girl Scouts.

This is more than just being a good girl who sells cookies. In fact, if there's a misconception about being a Girl Scout, it's that she's annoyingly perfect. Actually, the true Girl Scout is flawed like all of us, but trying and succeeding in our confusing, thorny, miraculous, real world. Being a Girl Scout is about being whoever you are, learning to do new things, and excelling, not so much in one subject, but in your own life. The soul of Girl Scouts is the same as its founder. Daisy was not the typical good girl with the ideal life. She got into trouble and was very outspoken. Her personal trials included becoming nearly deaf and marrying badly. But she moved beyond those difficulties to become an unusual and powerful role model for millions of girls.

Like many former Girl Scouts and mothers of Girl Scouts, until recently I knew Juliette Gordon Low's name and just a bit about her, but little else. A few years ago, with a group of neighborhood parents, I stood on the corner in front of a big brown Victorian on a Madison, Wisconsin, fall morning. I waved good-bye to the school bus taking our kindergartners, including my older daughter Eve, away to their world. My mind swam with the need to find my youngest daughter Julia's green froggy boots and just one set of crayons.

My new neighbor, Dana, broke my household reverie. "Would Eve like to join the Girl Scouts?"

We'd moved in the week before, a month late for kindergarten and not knowing anyone in town. After spending most of my life in Washington, DC, then two years in Denver, Colorado, we'd moved to this Midwest college town, to a neighborhood where we could walk to parks, coffee shops, and the zoo, and where my husband would practice cardiology. It sounded like a good life, and it was, but it would take time to build it, to make it our home. My job had shifted from full-time writer to part-time writer to manager of getting our lives back on track. Dana's question was an invitation to a community. Like many places in the country, Girl Scouts is a really big deal here. Girl Scouts. Yes. Thank you.

At the end of that school year, the college students running Eve's Girl Scout Daisy troop (the name for the youngest Girl Scouts) told us they were moving on, and that the leadership would need to be taken over by parents, or the troop would disband. Melissa and Sherry, two of the other moms, and I decided we'd take on the troop. How hard would it be with three of us? We are all moms of all girls. Melissa and Sherry each have three girls and I have two. The way girls talk and move and laugh and live is a part of our homes and every moment of our consciousness. Melissa is a champion of the underserved and the underdog, running her own nonprofit law firm in Madison. Sherry is a historian and former curator at the Circus World Museum in Baraboo, Wisconsin, which is where the Ringling Bros. Circus was founded. They are both athletic and funny, and are the kind of strong women friends you are glad you've found. Melissa has said sometimes she forgets to email me about something because we communicate telepathically. When we are running a meeting with the girls, our twelve different, wonderful girls, we can convey so much to each other without even speaking. We share a wavelength, a common language.

Because I am a reporter at heart and because I'm intensely curious (some would say nosy), I love to read and research and question things and people I find interesting. I needed to know about the dairy history of Madison and its Vietnam-era protests before moving; I will often cook food from a vacation spot like South Carolina or Tokyo or New Orleans before and after a visit. So as I began to lead this troop and think back to my own Girl Scout memories (my 1970s-era Girl Scout Brownie uniform and our handmade sit-upons stood out),

I searched and read and asked. I watched as the girls proudly earned petal after petal on their Girl Scout Daisy vests, eventually forming the whole flower. At one of our early meetings, we celebrated Founder's Day, October 31, Juliette Gordon Low's birthday, by singing "Happy Birthday" and opening a wrapped box we filled with foam cut-out petals that read the parts of the Girl Scout Law that we would work on that year: "Honest and Fair," "Friendly and Helpful," and the rest.

Still, my biggest, most burning, and unanswered questions were…*Who was Daisy? Who was Juliette Gordon Low?* Why did she decide to start the Girl Scouts? I was blown away that an organization started one hundred years ago could have such meaning for my life and that of my daughters. I felt that Daisy's individual personality wove through what we were learning and doing, and I wanted to know more about her.

As the American founder of the Girl Scouts in 1912, Daisy was not a household name among my friends. Books about her were outdated, hard to find, and definitely not in the mainstream of publishing. How could this be? My daughter and her troopmates might know every detail about a *Harry Potter* character, but they didn't even know that their troop was called "Daisy" based on Juliette Low's nickname. She got that durable name soon after she was born when one of her uncles said: "I bet she's going to be a daisy!"

When I realized information about Daisy was so difficult to find, my reporter instincts kicked in. I was now incredibly intrigued by how Daisy created a new girls club and what it continues to mean to the American woman. And that is how I became fascinated—obsessed—with Juliette Gordon Low. I wanted to know her story and tell it to the girls. When I decided to write about Daisy and tell her tale, it was clear my first stop would be, of course, where she was born.

I traveled to Savannah to walk around Daisy's childhood home, and to touch and read her hand-written letters at the Georgia Historical Society. British Lady Nancy Astor once described Savannah as "a pretty woman with a dirty face," which is apt. Savannah is a gorgeous city with more going on than what you can see at first glance. I later went to New York, to the Girl Scout Headquarters on 5th Avenue, wearing my temporary guest pass, and ensconced myself in a library on the seventeenth floor near the climate-controlled archives to dive into more letters and photos. I was in for a surprise. Her life was more interesting than I could have imagined. My trips to research Daisy's life were interspersed with our own troop meetings, where, as always, I continued to learn from the girls. As I was researching Girl Scout history, I was also living it in real time.

Daisy was a prolific letter-writer: to her parents, siblings, friends, and acquaintances. That was, of course, the way people communicated then, and news was very old by the time it got through. A letter with lots of information or big news was often requested to be sent on to others (no copying all as in emails). Sometimes, paper was in short supply and a writer would scrawl with her fountain pen on top of another letter, making the inky cursive more difficult to understand. At least once, Daisy instructed the recipient to "burn this letter" after it was read. After reading scores of her letters, I felt I knew Daisy better, having watched her handwriting change from that of a teenager away at school to that of an independent widow. She often drew little pictures and had a sense of humor, and her letters were rife with spelling errors. There is a sadness to many of her letters, sometimes stemming from a family death, but also from her loneliness and difficulty in finding her way for many years. Many of her later letters, after the Girl Scouts was founded, are brimming with joy and pride of accomplishment.

I learned that Daisy grew up in the deep South, and she was four years old when the Civil War ended. She later became partially deaf in one ear and then completely deaf in the other (bizarrely, by a grain of rice thrown at her at her own wedding). Her husband eventually would meet another woman and ask Daisy for a divorce. But before the divorce was final, he died, and Daisy found herself middle-aged, childless, and without a real purpose in life. An introduction at a luncheon and ensuing friendship with Sir Robert Baden-Powell, the founder of the Boy Scouts, encouraged her to found the Girl Scouts when she was in her fifties. Daisy was never a sweet young lady or, in later life, a sweet old lady. She said what was on her mind (usually loudly because she couldn't hear) and got in people's way, but she got things done. She was a southern belle with an independence of spirit that both landed her in messes and endeared her to her true friends. She was dramatic, imperfect, and definitely not a saint. She was real.

Daisy's English Regency–style home in Savannah—where she was born, raised, and held her wedding reception—was saved from demolition, bought, and restored by the Girl Scouts in the 1950s to be a Girl Scout National Program Center. The Juliette Gordon Low Birthplace looks just the way it did in 1886, the year of Daisy's wedding, and is now a stunning National Historical Landmark, the first to be named in the city. About sixty-five thousand people make the pilgrimage every year to what is known as "The Birthplace."

When Daisy threw herself into one of her unusual endeavors, nothing stopped her. When she learned blacksmithing, she created new wrought-iron front gates for her house. She worked so hard, she needed different clothes to make room for her newly formed muscles. With her animals all around (she loved dogs both large and small, parrots, and would take in many stray animals) and her antics (such as standing on her head in a meeting to show off the latest Girl Scout uniform shoes), Daisy became a treasured friend to the first Girl Scouts, much like a quirky fairy godmother. Daisy taught the girls to have fun, but at the same time gave them real life lessons, encouraging them to be self-sufficient and smart, and to stand up for themselves. She loved games, and turned every teachable moment into an enjoyable one as well. Daisy saw that girls individually became stronger when they worked collaboratively.

Daisy worked hard for the Girl Scouts, and what she received in return was a purpose and a passion that was put to incredibly good use. In every woman's life, there comes a time when she wonders what she should have done differently and whether it's too late to make a change. For Daisy, that moment was in 1911 when she was widowed, childless, in her fifties, and completely unsure of what to do with her life. It was then that she met Sir Robert Baden-Powell and began work with the Girl Guides in Scotland and London. It was far from too late for her, as she then brought the movement to the United States in the following year.

When I first went to "visit" Daisy, I boarded a plane from Madison to Savannah, not really knowing what I would find in her southern hometown, amongst letters and furniture, rumors of ghosts looming in the dining room, and descendants who might not want to field my questions. Walking around her lovely courtyard under the Spanish moss, touching the iron gates Daisy made herself, I thought that what is most lasting—the true legacy—is the sheer inspiration of this woman who has affected so many others. The gates are a wonder. It must have taken enormous strength to create them, as well as artistic skill to shape the detailed flowers, letters, and decorations.

I climbed up and down her stairs, peered through her windows, and felt simpatico with what she wanted to do. While I would not say a ghost accompanied me, I did feel like I was connecting with Daisy. And when I met her great-grandnephew, he was full of southern charm. I saw the houses, restaurants, and streets described with perfect pitch in what Savannahians call "The Book," *Midnight in the Garden of Good and Evil* by John Berendt. One afternoon, weddings popped up in every one of the gorgeous squares I walked through. There are twenty-two in the city—with names like Telfair, Oglethorpe, Ellis, Wright, and Lafayette, which is right across from the house Daisy lived in after she was married. The brides in their different—but all white—dresses walked down the cobblestone paths under big oak trees, and I wondered what Daisy thought on her wedding day, what she mused about when she walked across the street to Lafayette Square, if she stopped at a bench or met a friend for a stroll.

I thought about how Daisy's world was so different in many ways one hundred years ago, but how so many values she held dear—responsibility and being good to others—are those we place importance on today. I want the girls of my two daughters' generation to have even more opportunities than I have had; I want them to be strong and smart, to have good friends, and to have a good time. It is amazing to me to think about how women one hundred years ago wanted the same things for their daughters, nieces, and young friends. But at the same time, Daisy's championing of young women paved the way for a much more equitable world today. In her day, I probably wouldn't have been hired as a columnist for the business section at the *Washington Post,* let alone at age twenty-eight. My female friends who are inventors, executives, professors, and doctors would not have had the same opportunities they do now. What I have learned from Daisy is to hang on to and preserve the things that really matter and let the rest simply fall away. It is interesting to study Daisy now; we can learn from role models throughout history about living today. We are constantly bombarded by the up-to-the-minute version of technology or the latest clothing style. Sometimes there is value in looking at the old and adapting it to the new, taking lessons that speak to our core values and making them work for us.

While I was in Savannah I was constantly thinking about our troop at home and how much the
girls would love to know more about Daisy, too.
My third-grade daughter's troop is a picture of the
modern Girl Scouts. We troop leaders take them
on field trips, help them make holiday gifts (from
homemade hot chocolate to handmade cake
plates), and go on overnight campouts. But we,
like Daisy, are far from perfect. I am, sadly, afflicted
with a chronic bad sense of direction, not the best
attribute for a Girl Scout leader. When we drive to
a new location for an activity, I inevitably get lost,
and the girls make fun of me. Once, Melissa and
I were driving around in two separate cars, unsuc-
cessfully trying to find an ice skating rink where
the girls would have a lesson. Eventually we pulled
up next to each other on a country road, having
completely lost our way in the same spot. Luckily,
we were able to call Sherry, who reeled us in.

I really, really don't like to iron (and badges
need to be ironed, unfortunately), and I am very
bad at it. I'm the rare person who prefers the
sew-on badges to the iron-on. But I once spent
many hours ironing on troop numbers and our
council's name on each of our girls' Girl Scout
Brownie sashes to get them ready for their

bridging ceremony. The sashes were the first—and probably the last—things I've ironed that didn't look worse after I'd finished. The girls thought I should get a badge for doing it. There is comedy in it all—getting terribly lost, the lice outbreak that resulted in many of our girls taking on a pulled-back, slightly oiled hairstyle indicative of the anti-lice shampoo, the pumpkin patch breakdowns, the cookie selling competitions. But this troop, which started when they were kindergartners and will continue as long as they want (I'm so hoping they'll have each other through high school), has already become a sisterhood.

Several years into leading the group now, Melissa and Sherry and I have become close too. We are intensely aware of each others' schedules, trips, obligations, and milestones with our other kids and work and life. We have bounced hundreds of emails among the three of us about permission slips, checks, scheduling, choosing activities, and picking up art supplies. We push ourselves to encourage the girls to make more decisions on their own as they get bigger, to challenge them to try new things. We let them know we are on their side, they are not alone, and we and the other girls are their sisters. My older daughter will bridge from Girl Scout Brownie to Girl Scout Junior this year, and my younger daughter is a Girl Scout Daisy now, so I personally look forward to the years, and moments, ahead.

This book is not a traditional biography. It is a combination of historical stories about Daisy, current experts' advice and ideas, and my own experiences and inspiration as a Girl Scout. Yes, as a volunteer troop leader, I am, in my early forties, officially a Girl Scout again. Feel free to make fun of that—I'm having a fabulous time. The ten chapters of the book are not from an official Girl Scout list. They are simply what I think about most when I feel inspired by Daisy and her lessons, and see the girls in our troop living her legacy.

Of course, the very existence of Girl Scouts is not the answer to everything. Yet in these crazy, high-tech, yet disconnected times, the simple beliefs and tenets of Girl Scouts give girls a sense of belonging and a beautiful path to follow. The journey begun by Daisy is continued, every day, by these girls. These are the women of our next generation.

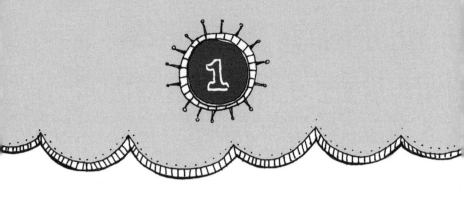

know yourself and be yourself

"Scouting rises within you and inspires you to put forth your best."

— Daisy in *The Rally* magazine, January 1919

Daisy Gordon was four years old when General William Tecumseh Sherman, the Yankee man she had heard was the devil, came to her house in Savannah, put her on his lap, and gave her and her sister rock candy, the first sugar she had ever tasted. Her father was away fighting against Sherman's army, so it was quite a shock to her to have this man walk through the front door of her house, bearing gifts for the kids, no less.

The Civil War, a persistent backdrop to Daisy's early childhood, had begun about six months after she was born on October 31, in 1860. The Union Army, clad in blue uniforms, marched through the streets singing, "When This Cruel War is Over." It was a war that divided the nation and split Daisy's own family. Daisy's mother, Nellie Kinzie Gordon, was from one of the founding families of Chicago, and Nellie's brothers were Union soldiers. But Daisy's father was a Confederate officer, slave owner, and cotton factor who bought and sold cotton. Sherman was a friend of Nellie's family, and after the surrender of Savannah he came to personally deliver letters from her family.

Daisy was not thrilled to see him—she supported her father. She was a southern girl in the way she dressed, spoke, and felt. Savannah—in its warm, wilting beauty—truly defined her. Just as her mother's family was prominent in the North, Daisy's father's family was well known in the South. Daisy's paternal grandfather, William Washington Gordon I, was a former mayor of Savannah and had also been the founder of the Central of Georgia Railroad, as well as the first graduate of West Point to come from Georgia.

After Savannah surrendered, Sherman presented the city, originally settled and planned by James Edward Oglethorpe, with its cobblestone streets, carefully designed squares, enormous fountains, and persistent ghost stories, as a Christmas present to President Abraham Lincoln.

Sherman ordered the evacuation of all families of Confederate officers, so Nellie and her children traveled to Chicago to stay with her family until the war ended. But even there, Daisy remained a southern girl. When word came in 1865 that her side had officially lost, the neighbors all came out for a parade by torchlight; Daisy climbed a fence, sat atop a gatepost and forcefully sang "Dixie," as a surprised crowd looked on, listened, and then continued their celebration.

Oh, I wish I was in the land of cotton,
Old times there are not forgotten,
Look away, look away, look away Dixie Land.

In Dixie Land, where I was born in,
early on one frosty mornin',
Look away, look away, look away Dixie Land.

I wish I was in Dixie, Hooray! Hooray!
In Dixie Land I'll take my stand
to live and die in Dixie.
Away, away, away down south in Dixie.
Away, away, away down south in Dixie

By Daniel Decatur Emmett, 1859

In Illinois, the children saw snow for the first time and ate foods that were not familiar to them back home. Although Daisy would later have a privileged, wealthy upbringing, during these early years in the South, she and her siblings were malnourished and the family stressed by wartime. Safe in Chicago, Daisy grew to understand that her northern relatives were her family too. Daisy's grandmother Juliette Magill Kinzie was a writer who published several books, including *Wau-Bun*, the story of pioneer life in Fort Winnebago, Wisconsin. She and her husband, John Kinzie, formed the first settlements in Chicago. At their home, as Daisy recovered from brain fever, a life-threatening illness, they told her many stories. One of her favorites was about her great-grandmother, Eleanor Lytle Kinzie. As a small girl of nine, Eleanor had been kidnapped by the Seneca Indians. The story goes that the tribe considered Eleanor as one of their own children and that the head of the tribe, Chief Cornplanter, named her "Little-Ship-Under-Full-Sail," because she moved so quickly and fearlessly. She lived with them as an adopted daughter for four years until Eleanor's parents finally convinced Chief Cornplanter to let them see their child. When Eleanor ran into her mother's arms, Chief Cornplanter saw how much her family missed her and let the girl return to her home. Daisy's family, where she was the second of six children, decided that she, too, fit that description, and , in addition to the nickname Daisy, she proudly took on the title of "Little-Ship-Under-Full-Sail."

That name encapsulates how Daisy led her life. It was in these early experiences that she first learned

JULIETTE GORDON LOW, AGE 10.

that even members of her own family had different ways of doing things. Later, when she was older, Daisy visited her friend Abby Lippitt Hunter and her family in Providence, Rhode Island. According to a remembrance called "Juliette Gordon Low

Grown-Up" by her niece Daisy Gordon Lawrence, she wrote back home: "I learn new things every day. I am in a family here who are different from anything I have seen before; in some respects their ideas and methods seem better than ours. It is rather narrow to condemn people because they differ from you…I am going to stop moralizing because I do it in bad spelling and I know that aggravates you."

Throughout Daisy's life as she was recognized for leadership, humor, and empathy, she was also known for being a terrible speller. Her mother tried to point it out in letters that included a little chart of Daisy's spelling compared to the correct way, in words such as "sleaves," "disgrase," "suspence," and "idear." In an 1871 letter, Daisy's mother wrote to her: "Please remember also that a persons bust means both their bosoms, and according to your description of Alice's 'busts' the unfortunate child has four—two in front I suppose and two behind I conclude which is certainly more than her share and I don't wonder her dress had to be let out."

Another particular quirk of Daisy's was her driving. Although she had money to buy a car and learned to drive before many people of her generation, she was known for having accidents and numerous near-misses. Once she crashed through a house, driving right into a dining room where a family was eating dinner. She didn't say a word to them, but went nearby to a telephone to call for help. "I didn't think it would be polite to interrupt them while they were eating," Daisy's brother Arthur Gordon recounts her saying then. She also had a habit of driving on the wrong side of the road as she moved back and forth from the U.S. to England and Scotland, which certainly contributed to her car troubles.

Daisy's brother Arthur described her in a

THE GORDON CHILDREN WHEN DAISY WAS ABOUT FIFTEEN YEARS OLD. CLOCKWISE FROM FRONT LEFT: MABEL, ELEANOR, DAISY, ARTHUR, BILL AND ALICE.

remembrance entitled "Juliette Gordon Low as Her Family Knew Her" by G. Arthur Gordon: "Her mind did not work like that of the average person…Two and two by no means made four to her. They made anything she chose to imagine they made…There was nothing conventional or tepid or neutral about her."

Daisy was always a rule-breaker, though not in a spiteful way or in a manner that would hurt someone, other than possibly herself. She called her high school "Edge of Hell" instead of Edge Hill because she got into so much trouble. In January 1877, Daisy wrote to her mother from that boarding school:

> But, Mama, I can't keep all the rules, I'm too much like you. Imagine yourself when at school, on being asked to do something against the rules to have some fun, turning up the whites of your eyes with righteous indignation, clasping you hands across your bosom, and saying "How Wrong!" I'll keep the rule about studying after the light bell rings, about getting up in the morning too soon, and I'll keep clear of big scrapes, but little ones I can't avoid. For instance, last week I got up after the light bell and I and another girl went on the one-eyed French teacher's floor and told ghost

stories until about twelve when we quietly and stealthily returned. But, oh, how I suffered for it. The teachers, of course, found it out and the next evening when I went to get my medicine, I caught it! Miss Middleton (the governess on our floor), the drawing teacher, and Mrs. Morrison got after me. Everyone talked. They quoted the Bible and read passages out of the Prayer Book. I received it like an angel and I smiled a little sickly smile.

Sarah Louise Arnold, the former Dean of Simmons College and National President of the Girl Scouts in the 1920s, wrote a book first published in 1934 that is a beautiful little gold volume of poems and inspirational advice to Girl Scouts and leaders, titled *The Way of Understanding.* "Surely we were meant to be different, to sing different strains, and to give back different messages. Only let our message be the message of our very best self," she wrote.

All of these girls, in every one of these generations, have peer pressure as something in common. And it is remarkably liberating and comforting to know that the other girls feel this too.

In our troop, one of the mothers called me to say her daughter was feeling different, left out, not just in the troop but also in other parts of her life.

She liked to wear different colors than some of the girls, had shorter hair, and liked a movie that was not a favorite of others in the troop. Sherry, Melissa, and I decided to try to help the girl feel more welcome among her sister Girl Scouts by bringing up the issue directly, without naming names. I'll admit I was nervous—on our to-do list was to have a snack, do an art project, and have a profound discussion about differences in personalities and how great it is that we are not all alike.

It happened to be April Fools' Day, so we started the meeting with the three of us walking in with crazy, long hair extensions, announcing that Girl Scouts had made a change to the uniform, and we would all start wearing our hair exactly the same way. We looked ridiculous but no one was laughing. We

GIRL SCOUTS OF THE USA FACTS

Founded: March 12, 1912, by Juliette Gordon Low (Daisy) in Savannah, Ga., and chartered by the U.S. Congress on March 15, 1950

Headquarters: 420 5th Avenue, New York, NY, USA

Active Girl Scouts: 3.2 million (2.3 million girl members and 880,000 adult members who are mostly volunteers)

Number of Councils: 112 (in 50 states and the District of Columbia)

Alumnae Girl Scouts: 50 million

Employees at GSUSA Headquarters: 400

were met with horrified stares. A few started saying they didn't like it, did they have to…and then one girl piped up, "Is this an April Fools' joke?" They were so relieved that it was. It was a fun lead-in to how happy we are all that we aren't the same and how we learn from each other in our differences. We talked about how Juliette Gordon Low was different in so many ways—stubborn, found her calling later in life, couldn't hear well, encouraged girls to have careers and play sports—and how great that was for all of us. Daisy started the Girl Scouts as a place where you came as you were, and you felt comfortable being there, at any moment of your life.

Then we played "snowball." Each girl wrote on a piece of paper three things about herself (I wrote that I'm curious, have a terrible sense of direction, and love olives). The girls crumpled their papers into balls, threw them into the center of the room, and then picked up another girl's paper. We took turns reading each out loud and had to guess who wrote them. They chose to reveal things such as liking Barbies and horses, not liking pink, being afraid of snakes, and being fast runners. We talked about how to respect each others' likes and dislikes, by not saying, "Yuck," if there is a difference of opinion but being able to say they just have another favorite movie or color.

Starting this lesson, Sherry, Melissa, and I thought we might have to do most of the talking, but instead the girls did, one by one, as the others were fascinated by their comments. The kids continued the conversation over cheese and crackers, raising their hands to reveal how they'd felt bad once when someone made fun of them for speaking a certain language in another country, or for liking a certain book. They could not get enough of discussing how they felt about differences. While the one girl who we originally were trying to help seemed happy and more comfortable than ever, it turned out each girl in the troop had an individual voice and opinion that day, which was welcomed and heard. It was a real-life example of something rising up within them that they might not have known was there—a common bond.

give to others

"Do a good turn daily."

— Scouting for Girls, the Official Handbook
of the Girl Scouts (1920)

When Daisy was a teenager, she and some of her friends and cousins, who lived next door in Savannah, formed a club called "Helpful Hands." Daisy had moved back to Savannah from Chicago in 1865. They rigged up a communication system using tin cans and string. As they were a family with both ideas and means, they also had their household servants send over messages, just to make sure they got through. Even at this early age, Daisy wanted the group to not just be a social club but to strive to make a difference. The club members had noticed that the children of the Italian family who ran a local fruit stall were dressed in shabby clothes, and it was decided that they would be the first beneficiaries of the Helpful Hands.

Taking the lead, Daisy gathered the club members and taught them how to sew, making clothes for the little children. Unfortunately, something went amiss in the sewing lessons. The children put on their new clothes, but almost immediately, the pink calico sleeves of one little boy's new outfit

JULIETTE GORDON LOW, CIRCA 1878.

fell off him as he ran through the street. Then, as Daisy remembers, the whole outfit came off: "The boy discarded the garment altogether and raced home sans culottes, pursued by the police-man." From then on, the group was known as the "Helpless Hands," according to Daisy's own recounting of the story in "When I was a Girl" by Juliette Low in the October 1926 issue of *The American Girl* magazine.

Later that year, a terrible yellow fever epidemic hit the city. Daisy, along with her mother and siblings, as well as many other people, fled Savannah.

But sadly, one of the Italian children and then one of the club members, a ten-year-old girl, died. Throughout her life, Daisy sought to help others. During the Spanish-American War in 1898, Daisy and her mother set up a hospital in Miami for American soldiers returning from Cuba. Daisy and her mother helped treat seventy to eighty patients at one time. Their efforts were lauded across the country, and people called Nellie the "Angel of the Boys in Blue."

Throughout her life, Daisy championed the less fortunate and comforted the afflicted, which would include the poor, sick, and animals of any kind. On the other hand, she did not have much patience or good will toward those who were boring or annoying, or prevented her from doing something she wanted to do. She also "…despised and loathed any form of meanness or trickery, and when she thought she detected it, her scorn was blazing and furious," remembers Daisy's brother, Arthur Gordon, in a 1935 address to a Girl Scout conference in Richmond, Virginia.

In the spirit of Daisy's desire to give to others, it has been a tradition for Girl Scouts to do service projects, which range from small but significant one-time efforts to longer-term endeavors. During

DAISY PETALS

Daisy petals are colored badges earned by the youngest Girl Scouts that form a daisy. Each has a "Flower Friend" name.

* **Blue Center:** Learn the Girl Scout Promise
* **Light Blue:** Honest and Fair (Lupe the Lupine)
* **Yellow:** Friendly and Helpful (Sunny the Sunflower)
* **Spring Green:** Considerate and Caring (Zinni the Zinnia)
* **Red:** Courageous and Strong (Tula the Tulip)
* **Orange:** Responsible for what I Say and Do (Mari the Marigold)
* **Purple:** Respect Myself and Others (Gloria the Morning Glory)
* **Magenta:** Respect Authority (Gerri the Geranium)
* **Green:** Use Resources Wisely (Clover)
* **Rose:** Make the World a Better Place (Rosie the Rose)
* **Violet:** Be a Sister to Every Girl Scout (Vi the Violet)

World War I, girls sewed clothes and canned food for the military. A troop in Washington, DC, came up with a way to battle influenza, making ten gallons of broth daily to give to poor, anemic children on the playgrounds during the winter. They sold Liberty Bonds and planted "victory gardens," full of vegetables and herbs. While Girl Scouts have found they are especially needed during wartime, they also work hard to help individual people or families or groups in many kinds of trouble. In later years Girl Scouts have collected litter, knit for the Red Cross, and given toys to needy children. They've volunteered with elderly people, taught kids with disabilities, and have accomplished so many other projects that embody the generous spirit. Sarah Louise Arnold writes about true generosity in her parable about "a handful more," putting in just a bit more sugar in your rhubarb pie or your effort to help someone, than you might think you can. In her book *The Way of Understanding*, she writes: "'Your rhubarb pie is powerful good, Neighbor. It isn't the least bit sharp or sour as so many pies are. I wonder how you make it.' The neighbor smiled and said, 'When I make rhubarb pie I put in all the sugar I think I can afford, and then I shut my eyes and put in a handful more.'"

The giving spirit is vitally alive in the volunteer structure of the Girl Scouts, which is the largest volunteer organization for women and girls in the United States. When you think about it, volunteering is really giving of yourself. While there are several hundred Girl Scout employees, there are hundreds of thousands more unpaid workers who are troop leaders, counselors, and drivers. Multitudes of jobs keep the groups running, and the girls engaged and interested. Many of these volunteers are locally based. Some are mothers, grandmothers, and fathers of the Girl Scouts. The Girl Scouts simply would not be possible without these volunteers. As in many types of gratifying work, the worker gains enormous amounts from the experience too. They give, but they receive, many times over.

When I first signed on to be a troop leader, I did not have any inkling of how much it would eventually mean to me. First, it is incredible time with my own daughter. She's still at the age (I hope this lasts at least a bit longer) where she wants me around, and she's proud that I'm one of her leaders. She likes the insider information about what craft or field trip is coming up. I also love seeing her interact with her friends. Those of you who have volunteered at your kids' schools or coach their teams or have been involved with their other activities know what I mean. It's wonderfully eye-opening to watch how they work out problems and talk with each other.

What I learn from this group of twelve is amazing. I love hearing their different ways of looking at the world and, several years into it, watching them change and grow up. It is a commitment. We're ice skating together in the winter, swimming in the summer, driving the kids all around, and often cutting out small pieces of felt for art projects. There are times when they don't listen to us, when they don't like a craft we've chosen, and when we are worried because one of them accidentally got on the school bus instead of coming to the meeting. By the end of some meetings, Melissa and Sherry and I look at each other and smile, exhausted, happy we've pulled it off. But—and this is the absolute truth—at every event, meeting, or hour with these girls, there is fun and there is meaning. That's the ideal volunteer job, learning from each other and having a great time.

I have worked enough in different jobs to know that, paid or unpaid, having work where you are able to do the kinds of things you want to do and are recognized for it, is rare. For us, recognition is not financial and is mostly in the form of smiles and thank-yous. The parents send us nice notes and even (unnecessarily but appreciated) a gift card at the end of the year. The kids will often say they had fun doing something, and we can, even more often, see that they are. We can tell that the parents and girls are grateful for us, and we are for them. Some of our troop parents help by teaching a certain skill, by running to get juice and water during an event, or in many other ways. Most importantly, they are supporting their daughters by encouraging them to be in Girl Scouts.

Our troop has collected toys and money for Haiti earthquake victims, and donated from our cookie sales to preserve Daisy's house in Savannah. We have also raised money for the "Cookie Share" program, where customers donate money toward boxes of cookies that are then distributed at food pantries in our area. These are things the troop takes seriously. There is in these girls a natural desire to help others, especially children and animals.

While altruism can be innate, it can also be helpful to study successful models of giving and community service. Many of the parents in our group and our friends in Madison are particularly interested in one of the most vital issues—childhood hunger and the quality of the food our children eat. I am a big fan of Billy Shore, the founder of Share Our Strength, the nonprofit dedicated to ending childhood hunger, and chair of Community Wealth Ventures. Shore and his sister Debbie Shore started Share Our Strength—SOS—in 1984 in his Washington, DC basement, during the Ethiopian famine. They hoped to improve the way the world is fed. When I asked Shore why it is, intrinsically, that we need to give to others, he said humans are programmed to leave something good behind, to do something that really counts. Giving money is obviously helpful and important, but contributing thoughts, time and talent—what Daisy and Girl Scout leaders have done for one hundred years—is invaluable. "What I love about finding ways for people to share their strengths, as the Girl Scouts do, is that unlike those who write checks and suffer donor fatigue, when you are contributing through your unique value added, there is no burn-out," he said. "It's sustainable."

On a smaller scale here in Wisconsin, many of us are focusing on making sure our own families have dinner together and are working toward improving school lunches and snacks for all the kids in the district; an enterprise that sounds easy yet is very complex on many levels. We're lucky in Wisconsin to have so many great farmers who grow delicious food and give us a clear picture of where our food comes from, and help us in a "Farm to School" program.

Our troop's most memorable service project so far is one that we hope will be ongoing. On a beautiful spring afternoon, we picked up the girls, packed them into our three cars, and drove them just a few minutes away to Neighborhood House; a community center designed for everyone in our area, whether they are affluent, in need, or anything in between. It is a place where so many things go on, it is almost dizzying. There is a one-room high school, packed with books and computers, for kids having trouble—mostly due to drugs or alcohol—in regular school. A huge gymnasium holds sports events, practices, and an all-ages movie and dinner night, where the film is projected on the wall. There's an art room, a kitchen, and a living room with couches and a pool table. We came that day to volunteer for the food pantry part of Neighborhood House. Most of our kids had heard about food pantries and had brought in cans and boxes for various drives, but had never been to one.

They grew silent looking at the high shelves filled with big bags of rice, cans of green beans, and giant containers of peanut butter. All were familiar foods to them, but it was clear from their silence that they knew they were lucky they could just grab some of those foods out of their own home cabinets. As our guide led us around, she explained how people are often embarrassed to come to the pantry, and she has to encourage them to take enough food for their families. It is hard, she explained, for people to ask for help sometimes. Very few people take more than they need, she said. They are, mostly, honest and fair. The kids listened and then moved from silence to questions as we began our first project—tackling the dozens of cardboard boxes the food had arrived in, breaking them down and putting them in a recycling bin. They wanted to see the enormous pot used for group dinners, wanted to know how people found out where the food pantry was, and if children came with their parents.

The chatter of good questions and answers continued as we moved on to sign-making. We needed to make signs—in English and in Spanish—to direct people to the right door for the food pantry, and to give them the hours of operation. We put poster board and papers down on the floor of the big gymnasium, split them into groups, and let them create. The girls colored the signs with bright markers and fun designs. The signs were informative and cheery, and had the sweet markings of little hands that mean well. The signs were hung on the doors and windows at Neighborhood House, and the girls saw they made a little bit of change in someone's life. They also understood that the work that day was not all about them. We often in our troop make projects or crafts the girls get to keep. But we also create gifts for others, and we learn that when we give our time and abilities, we may not leave with a thing, but instead a memory, and a feeling of doing something good.

love living things

"Girl Scouts learn that being kind to animals applies to these dwellers of woods and meadows as well as to dogs and cats, horses and cows."

—The Girl Scout Handbook, 1933

One day, when Daisy was a young boarding school student, she found a little robin frozen to death. She immediately set about making him a burial. She found a pasteboard box the shape of a coffin, put little silver pins around the sides, and even made the bird a shroud. Six friends acted as pallbearers; Daisy was the minister, speaking about the life and death of the tiny bird.

When Daisy was a little girl, she brought home a dead dog and tried to revive it, to no avail, according to the story "My Aunt Daisy was the First Girl Scout" by Arthur Gordon. Thankfully, not all of Daisy's animal stories ended so sadly. Gordon also recounts in his 1956 *Woman's Day* story that she once bought a baby rabbit from some children because she thought its ears were too cold. She put it on a hot water bottle and rubbed its ears until it warmed up to her satisfaction.

At one point, according to the remembrance "Juliette Low as Her Family Knew Her," by G. Arthur Gordon, Daisy requested she be fed with the animals in the barn instead of the people inside

JULIETTE GORDON LOW, CIRCA 1878.

the house, because she felt the animals were on a better schedule and she liked their company. Her father agreed, provided that she would milk his beloved Jersey cow Lilburn. But when Daisy forgot, she was sent back to eating with the humans.

One Thanksgiving, Daisy tried to save the turkey. She convinced her father to chloroform the turkey rather than cut its head off. So the bird was put to sleep, plucked, and stored in a cold room (they didn't have refrigerators in those days). But when the family cook opened the door to cook dinner, she found the turkey had woken up and was running around, giving everyone a big surprise (according to Daisy's nephew Arthur Gordon in "My Aunt Daisy Was the First Girl Scout," *Woman's Day*, March 1956).

All her life, Daisy was surrounded by animals. She felt great empathy for animals and greatly enjoyed their company. Over the years she had

JULIETTE GORDON LOW WITH HER PARROT, POLLY POONS, CIRCA 1895.

a beagle named Bow Wow, cats named Nox and Kittle, a parrot named Polly Poons, a Pekinese dog named Chiencapieu, and many others. She learned to ride horseback, which would become a regular part of her life in England.

When Daisy traveled on her first trip abroad in 1882, she became reacquainted with a handsome young man named William Low. He then visited her in Savannah, bringing Daisy a fox terrier as a present, as she adored animals. Her animals, and those of her family's, were always a powerful source of comfort to Daisy during both the good times and the bad, the latter of which included the death of her beloved sister Alice when the sisters were young women. From the earliest Girl Scout handbooks, there is advice about choosing and caring for a pet, focusing on the responsibility and education of taking care of a living being. Some editions give details on raising white mice, taming squirrels and chipmunks, and taking care of monkeys. "[Monkeys] are pets for older girls and for persons who understand them," according to the 1933 Girl Scout handbook.

Anybody who has ever had a pet, from a tadpole to a pot-bellied pig, knows that the bond between a human and her animal can be profound. This was certainly true for Daisy. Taking care of pets is proven to make us healthier, both mentally and physically. It's also been discovered that people who have dogs, specifically, get more exercise, because they walk with them. Interestingly, a University of Missouri

JULIETTE GORDON LOW, CIRCA 1882.

study found recently that people benefit more from walking with their dogs than with humans. The walkers' speed increased 28 percent with dogs and only 4 percent with people. The author of the study, Dr. Rebecca Johnson (*Walk a Hound, Lose a Pound,* 2011), also found people talked each other out of exercise or complained about the weather to avoid walking. The dogs were just happy to take a walk. Animals have been helping us for generations, and more people are now focused on "animal therapy" for those who have lost a family member, for law school students, who (at least at Yale) can check out a therapy dog at their library to help them work out stress, and for people who have autism. *The Horse Boy* by Rupert Isaacson is an incredible story of a father's quest to help his son through autism with the aid of horses. The life of Temple Grandin, an autistic woman who became an important animal behaviorist, is also inspiring and helps underscore the human-animal bond.

For some of us, a bevy of animals and a cacophony of natural sounds and activities is the best. For me, it's about having one dog. As an only child, my Welsh terrier, Sesame, who I had from ages four to seventeen, was like a sibling to me. We played in the yard together, went on walks, and she was always so happy to see us when we walked in the door. She died just as I was packing to go away to Boston University.

During the time I've been writing this book, our family welcomed Bebe, a tri-colored beagle. She is a companion for our daughters, but she is also great friend to me and my husband, a wonderful running partner, and source of great laughter in our house.

As I started looking at dog training options in Madison, I found that one of the country's most interesting thinkers on animal behavior was right in town: Patricia O'Connell. She is the author of *The Other End of the Leash: Why We Do What We Do around Dogs,* and *For the Love of a Dog: Understanding Emotions in You and Your Best Friend.* O'Connell recommends treating your dog's first week in the house as her first week on the job—all about learning rules, routines and culture. She writes in *For the Love of a Dog*:

> We've called dogs our best friends for centuries, and what is more basic to friendship than an emotional connection? A friendship with no emotional component is no friendship at all, it's a business arrangement (and even those usually have their share of emotional loading attached). Our dogs evoke a veritable sea of emotions in us, and we ride the waves back and forth between love and joy and sadness and anger almost on a daily basis.

That's the way Daisy felt about her animals— they were her true friends and companions. And in the years following, generations of Girl Scouts have followed Daisy's lead, forming emotional connections to the animals in our world, and valuing their existence in our lives.

When we asked our second grade troop what reward they would like for cookie-selling (using some of the troop money earned to do an activity or trip of their choice), they voted to go horseback riding together. They pulled the choice out of the air—we said they could suggest anything they could think of. So on a beautiful May morning, we traveled to a farm and stables just outside of Madison. Only one of the twelve girls had much experience with horses, and she had this advice: "All the horses have different personalities. Some buck, some are slower, and some are funny."

Each of six horses was assigned two girl riders, who would take turns on the horse. The girls first learned to brush the horses, gingerly getting to know them. It helped that they had names, such as Applejack and Tiffany. We found out they also had fancier names for their other job as show horses. One by one, the girls were

IMPORTANT DAYS OF THE YEAR FOR GIRL SCOUTS

* **Feb. 22**—World Thinking Day (Sir Robert Baden-Powell and Olave Baden-Powell's birthday)
* **March 12**—Girl Scout Birthday (anniversary of the first meeting on March 12, 2012)
* **April 22**—Leader Appreciation Day
* **Oct. 31**—Founder's Day (Daisy's birthday)

lifted up on "their" horses and trotted outside. A few of the horses started meandering into a meadow, but were brought back into the round fenced circle, where the girls learned more about their horse's personality. One girl found her horse a little slow and demanded, "Trot, trot, trot!" It didn't. Another girl's horse took off to a corner where it apparently wanted to trot around in small circles. Another was going fast, just really fast. Eventually, after coaching from the stable owner, the girls were smiling and riding through the warm breeze, distinctly individual girls on their unique horses.

A few months later, our group took an ecosystem walk through the Madison Arboretum. We talked about how living things, from bugs to horses, keep our worlds alive, and how we all need each other to survive. Sometimes, the animals are working when we don't even know it, like the bees collecting pollen and the bats getting rid of the mosquitoes as part of the natural food cycle. We decided to make a visit to a veterinarian's office, where we could learn more about how our cats and dogs and other house pets are cared for there, and thereby become better owners ourselves. We may not be able to speak the same language as our dogs or the grasshoppers in the lawn, but we can respect them and appreciate their beauty and usefulness.

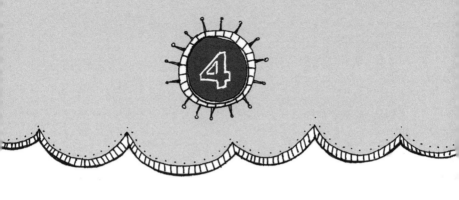

take care of yourself

"Health is probably a woman's greatest capital,
and a Girl Scout...doesn't waste it in poor diet...
so that she goes bankrupt before she is thirty.
Money is a very useful thing to have...A Girl
Scout saves, as she spends, on some system."

— Scouting for Girls, the Official Handbook
of the Girl Scouts (1920)

After a courtship in her mid-twenties, kept secret in part because her father did not approve, Daisy married William Mackay Low. She called him "Billow" because there were so many other Williams in her life, including her father and brother. In many ways, it seemed a perfect match—he was handsome, charming, and from a wealthy and prominent Savannah family. Billow's father, like Daisy's, was a cotton factor. But on the other hand, Billow did not work on his own to support himself. On

THE WEDDING BREAKFAST AFTER THE MARRIAGE CEREMONY OF WILLY LOW AND DAISY GORDON, DECEMBER 21, 1886, SAVANNAH, GEORGIA, TAKEN IN THE GARDEN OF THE JULIETTE GORDON LOW BIRTHPLACE.

their wedding day, the groom gave each of Daisy's ten bridesmaids a brooch of diamonds forming a Daisy with the year "1886" as a diamond stem, and presented Daisy herself with a crescent-and-star diamond pin. Billow was an authority on jewels, and always bought them loose and then had them set in designs he chose himself.

Daisy picked December 21 to commence her marriage at Christ Church, as it was her parents' anniversary, and they had always represented to her a committed and loving pair. The bridal bouquet was composed of lilies of the valley, which had been her sister Alice's favorite flower. Daisy's wedding dress was white silk trimmed with lace. A wedding breakfast, which is what they called a reception at the time, was held after the ceremony at Daisy's parents' house. The couple then left to honeymoon on St. Catherine's Island, off the coast of Georgia.

Billow's father, who had run a cotton business, died the summer before the wedding. Shortly after the honeymoon, the newlyweds moved overseas to England where the family business was located. Daisy and Billow set up home in England, eventually at Wellesbourne House in Warwickshire. The couple also regularly spent time in Scotland. In

Britain, the couple was welcomed into the social crowd of the Prince of Wales, who would later become King Edward VII of England.

Though the genteel British life was completely different from her southern upbringing, Daisy embraced her new world, riding horses, hunting, and attending glamorous balls and parties. Still, there were glimpses of the stubborn, eccentric Daisy. While in line to be presented to Queen Victoria in her court in 1889, Daisy became tired and—scandalously, to the onlookers—rested her bouquet of flowers on the bustle of the woman in front of her. Daisy did miss her family greatly. One familiar comfort to her was Savannah cooking. Daisy brought her cook, Mosianna Milledge, with her to London, and when Daisy held parties, she introduced traditional southern food, such as fried okra, black-eyed peas, and candied sweet potatoes to British royalty.

During this period, Daisy continued to devote much of her time to art. She was serious about her artwork, and took lessons to improve her skills. She loved to paint, draw, sculpt, and even do ironwork. It was then that she learned black smithing and forged the set of iron gates with intricate daisies and the initials of her parents; the gates stand at

BILLOW AND DAISY ON THEIR WEDDING DAY, DEC. 21, 1886.

her childhood home in Savannah today. Mostly, her life revolved around Billow's work and plans. They wanted to have children, but never did.

Daisy and Billow began spending more time apart in 1901. He was drinking and openly began spending time with a mistress, who Daisy knew as "Mrs. Bateman."

Daisy was completely devastated by Billow's abandonment of their marriage. Then, Billow asked Daisy for a divorce. It was a huge shock for her to have gone from complete emotional and financial dependence on her parents, to Billow, to being entirely by herself.

Although Daisy knew Billow had a mistress, one who was even at times staying with him in their home, she at first refused to believe it was the end of her marriage. She thought that somehow her husband would come to his senses and realize his mistake.

"I think Mrs. Bateman is likely to ruin Willie's married life and make it impossible for me to over-look his conduct, and then she is quite capable of chucking him. That is why I cabled[.] I wished to wait a year before consenting to any final measure. In that time, he ought to find her out," Daisy wrote to her father in January 1902.

Daisy did find at this time enormous support from her many friends and family. But she also found herself greatly embarrassed by the way her husband was blatantly carrying on this affair, and by how quickly the news was spreading. She continued in the letter to her father: "…what I feel is that he is absolutely cutting his own throat socially and morally and when I face the gossip etc. I feel as if my life was a nice clean garment which was being dragged through the mud."

Eventually, Billow became very ill, but he did not change his mind about Mrs. Bateman.

Daisy wrote a poem called "The Road" a few years later that encapsulated her feelings. These are the first few lines:

The road which led from you to me
Is choked with thorns and overgrown.
We walked together yesterday,
But now—I walk alone.

Like many women of her time, Daisy had no means of supporting herself, and no idea how to manage her finances. Even later, she was known for filing bills in envelopes marked "this year," "next year," "some time" and "never."

She wrote to her father asking for money as she corresponded with lawyers who negotiated a divorce settlement. Daisy was particularly annoyed that Billow was insisting on a clause that she not marry again, and she refused to agree to any deal that included that stipulation. She delayed the divorce as long as possible, at first because she thought he would change his mind and then through anger and resentment. Before the divorce was finalized, in 1905, Billow died. He had been very sick, but it was still a surprise. Then came the news that he had left his estate to Mrs. Bateman. Eventually, Daisy was able to win ownership of their house in Savannah and some money. After Billow's death (according to Daisy's sister Mabel) a parcel of letters between Billow and Mrs. Bateman were sent anonymously to Daisy, who would not read them. Those letters have disappeared, and some think they were eventually burned or destroyed.

Years after her husband left her, Daisy not only recovered personally, but went on to found and fund-raise for the Girl Scouts. She also became a steadfast voice for women's financial independence. From the highest profile women in the country to regular people in our everyday lives, we have seen that few of us expect a spouse to leave or die. Sometime in our lives, we all have to face the unexpected. While it is wonderful to lean on the person we love, we also have to build ourselves as strong women. Women are running companies, households and countries in greater number and more powerfully and effectively than in Daisy's day, but there is much more work to be done. Women still are earning about 25 percent less than their male counterparts. Women are also more likely to be living in poverty than men (White House Council on Women and Girls, 2011).

THIS PORTRAIT OF DAISY AT AGE TWENTY-SEVEN WAS PAINTED BY
EDWARD HUGHES JUST AFTER HER MARRIAGE TO BILLOW. THE ORIGINAL
NOW HANGS AT THE NATIONAL PORTRAIT GALLERY IN WASHINGTON, DC.

Daisy promoted more than just financial independence for women though. She also encouraged girls to know how to cook (they had to be
able to feed themselves and their families), be
physically fit, and wash their hands often, among
many other things. She gave them advice and
ideas about choosing a career, which was initially
met with criticism by many parents who thought
it was not a suitable subject for girls. "Scouting is

the cradle of careers. It is where careers are born," Daisy wrote in an undated document entitled "The History and Activities of Girl Scouts by Juliette Low, Founder of the Girl Scouts of America" [sic]. "These badges represent to a girl something that she has achieved and are a mark of progress. They often develop a taste and awaken an interest in some special subject which may lead a girl to find her future vocation." Daisy encouraged the girls to take care of themselves, in every way.

As long as there have been girls, there have been girls who struggle with their body image—their weight, skin, and type of hair. Daisy herself wrote home from boarding school to her mother that she was worried about her "ginormous" nose. The Girl Scouts, smartly, have addressed this issue consistently and aggressively. Pretending that it's not happening and ignoring the subject is not the way to improve girls' self-esteem. About 90 percent of teenage girls talk about their body shape and 86 percent of them think they should be on a diet, according to a recent Harvard University study. From the early days of Girl Scouts, Daisy's message was to eat well, exercise, and be happy with yourself the way you are. Of course, that's simple and useful advice, but not always so easy to follow.

In 2002, Girl Scouts began a relationship with Dove, the personal care brand of Unilever, creating the Girl Scout/Dove Self-Esteem Program, to empower girls ages eight to seventeen to feel better about themselves and to think about themselves as beautiful in all of their own ways. The *Uniquely Me* books that have come from that program emphasize the importance of being yourself and recognizing what is best about yourself.

The Girl Scouts organization has been actively involved in introducing the Healthy Media for Youth Act in Congress, which supports girl empowerment groups and promoting more balanced images of girls and women in the media. They did this after the Girl Scouts of the USA's Research Institute found that 89 percent of girls said that they feel pressure from the fashion industry to be thin. A related study in 2007 by the American Psychological Association found that three of the most common and life-threatening mental health issues for girls—eating disorders, depression, and low self-esteem—can be linked to the way women and girls are portrayed in the media. Actress Geena Davis, who has also been campaigning for the Healthy Media for Youth Act, found that male characters still outnumber female characters three to one in family films and television, and that only 27 percent of the speaking roles are given to females (Geena Davis Institute of Gender in Media, 2010).

The Girl Scouts emphasize self-compassion, which is slowly being rediscovered in our every-day lives. In our society we, rightly, place great importance on helping others and advising others what to do. But who takes care of the exhausted mother or the overworked executive? She has to take care of herself to even be able to give to others.

So many of us struggle with what we today call work-life balance. One of my favorite time-less books about women's lives is Anne Morrow Lindbergh's *Gift From the Sea.* It was written in 1955, but seems more relevant every time I re-read it. In it Lindbergh writes about the art of being alone, even for small moments, to recharge our-selves. "Even those whose lives had appeared to be ticking imperturbably under their smiling clock-faces were often trying, like me, to evolve another rhythm with more creative pauses in it, more adjustment to their individual needs, and new and more alive relationships to themselves as well as others," Lindbergh writes.

Self-compassion is part of what comes into play when girls learn about accepting themselves The Girl Scouts encourages girls to protect themselves, physically and emotionally. Girl Scouts today still run, swim, and play sports like tennis and basketball, just like the girls in the first troops. Girls today are also likely to try karate, yoga, and other methods of defense and relaxation. This is especially important because girls are prime targets for certain kinds of attacks. Electronic communication like texting, email, and social networking gives bullies a shield to hide behind when they are sending mean messages to their victims. While male students are more likely to be attacked with weapons, female students are twice as likely as males to be victims through electronic bullying, according to the 2011 White House Council Women in America report. We—as parents and Girl Scout leaders—are trying to move beyond just telling them to get off the computer by encouraging the kids to live in the real, rather than electronic, world for more of their days.

Bullying—electronic or not—is one of the biggest problems facing our families. Bullying will affect most of the children in our lives. A key theme in Girl Scouts is to build skills to be confident and stand up for yourself, abilities that will help when faced by bullies or the option of becoming a bully. It's also important for role models to talk about bullying. For her wedding, Kate Middleton chose as one of her charity registries an anti-bullying group; instead of sending her and Prince William wedding gifts, gift-givers could donate to Beatbullying.

The Girl Scout Research Institute, which studies girls' behavior, has become one of the leading sources of information about what kids are currently thinking. And it's a way the Girl Scouts has been able to stay important to kids through the years. As much as we do have genuine issues about our kids to worry about, it's interesting that a 2009 study of students in grades three through twelve by the Girl Scout Research Institute, entitled *Good Intentions: The Beliefs and Values of Teens and Tweens Today*, found that kids today are really trying to make a better life for themselves:

> Generally speaking, youth today are intent on making responsible choices, respecting others, and engaging in their communities and civic life. In several ways, it is youth who are charting a new direction for the country—towards personal and public responsibility. Additionally, it is important that adults understand how they can be supportive in this process, as youth look to the adults in

their lives to an even greater degree than they did a generation ago.

Some of what is important in these findings is that the kids clearly want to do well, but sometimes they need help finding the right answers to their questions, or need guidance in following through.

These findings are especially interesting, because the Institute had done a similar study in 1989 and could compare results twenty years later. The modern kids are, among other things, more likely than the kids were two decades ago to be accepting of a gay or lesbian friend, to think smoking is a bad idea, to intend to wait until marriage to have sex, to refuse a drink at a party, and to not cheat on a test. The kids are not entirely all right, but they are trying. We—the moms—are not perfect either. But the girls are watching, and sometimes emulating. We all need role models. Accepting being not perfect is a huge lesson for them and for us. In 2008, another Girl Scouts study found that there is a "close alliance between mothers' own ambitions and outlook on life with their daughters' aspirations and motivations."

What has become one of the most iconic images of Girl Scouts—selling cookies—continues in every generation to be a modern day lesson about finances and the value of work and making a living. The first Girl Scout cookies sold to support troop activities date back to 1917, when the cookies were homemade by Girl Scouts and their families. A 1922 article in *The American Girl* magazine suggests a plan from Miss Florence E. Neill of Chicago, in which girls can make cookies in big batches and then sell them for a profit. She recommended wrapping the cookies in wax paper bags and selling two cookies for five cents or a dozen cookies for twenty-five or thirty cents.

All over the country, Girl Scouts came up with different ways to sell cookies to support their troops. In 1926, Girl Scouts in Indianapolis organized the first large-scale cookie sale, selling thousands of cookies and making $662.79 to fund a new recreation hall at their camp. In 1934, the Girl Scouts of Greater Philadelphia became the first council to sell commercially made cookies. In 1935, the Girl Scout Federation of Greater New York (including Manhattan, Brooklyn, Bronx, Queens, and Staten Island councils) bought its own die to cut cookies in a trefoil shape, and advertised "Girl Scout Cookies" on the box they sold them in.

By 1948, demand for the cookies had grown so exponentially that the Girl Scouts had licensed twenty-nine commercial bakeries to officially produce the cookies. Since then, the girls have only stopped selling cookies one time, during World War II, when there was a flour, butter, and sugar shortage. Today, there are just two bakeries that produce up to eight varieties of cookies, including the three must-haves (they are required to produce these super popular cookies): thin mint, peanut butter sandwich, and shortbread—and then can choose others to manufacture.

But even something as seemingly sweet and innocent as the Girl Scout cookie has come under fire, and questions surrounding the cookies (their ingredients, environmental impact, health concerns) have ignited several controversies. The Girl Scouts have addressed these issues by experimenting with different packaging, for example, reducing paperboard waste by 150 tons in a recent year just on sales of one variety of cookie. They have also experimented with healthier cookie options and added the option of purchasing a "Cookie Share," which is both a service fund-raiser and clever option for those who don't want to eat cookies. The Girl Scouts even launched an iPhone app,

THE FIRST GIRL SCOUT COOKIE RECIPE

This homemade cookie recipe appeared in the July 1922 issue of the Girl Scout's magazine, *The American Girl*, and seems to be one of the first records of how Girl Scout cookie-selling began. It was suggested that girls could make and sell cookies to raise money for their troops, selling the cookies for twenty-five or thirty cents per dozen or five cents for two cookies. After rolling thin, the girl baker probably cut them in circles using a cookie cutter or small can.

* 1 cup butter
* 1 cup sugar
* 2 tablespoons milk
* 2 eggs

* 1 teaspoon vanilla
* 2 cups flour
* 2 teaspoons baking powder

Cream butter and sugar, add well-beaten eggs, then milk, flavoring, flour, and baking powder. Roll thin, sprinkle sugar on top, and bake in quick oven.

Makes 6 or 7 dozen cookies

called "The Cookie Finder," where people can type in their zip code and find the nearest source of Thin Mints, Caramel deLites, (Samoas), Trefoils, or Lemonades. Millions of people have downloaded it, according to the Girl Scouts, and found their cookies that way.

When we set out to teach our girls how to sell cookies, it felt like setting up a small business with twelve CEOs. Their different, wonderful personalities emerged in so many ways. Some wanted to win, to sell the most, and to get the best prizes. Others were really excited about the social aspect, going door-to-door to houses they knew, and maybe seeing some friends. There were girls who were a little nervous about it, and those who were most interested in the types of cookies and, of course, tasting them. We saw there were girls who were particularly gifted at presentation, who spoke well and explained clearly the cookie options, prices, and method of delivery.

That first year of selling cookies we decided to do role playing, so the girls could act out what would happen when they went door-to-door. First, we made sure of their safety. They had to have an adult with them, and they were never to go inside a stranger's house.

In the hallway outside the classroom where we meet, we put masking tape on the floor to make squares to serve as "houses." One girl would stand inside (the potential customer) and another (the Girl Scout cookie salesperson) would "ring" the doorbell. The customer girls wore costumes and necklaces (we were going to use hats, but an unfortunate lice epidemic was afflicting our troop). Each seller would "knock" on the customer's door, and the customer would read from a card. The kids loved acting out cookie selling. A customer saying, "Oh, I don't really like cookies," was encouraged to donate to the "Cookie Share" program—where they could donate cookies to other people. They learned to help people decide among cookie varieties and to mention that the cookies freeze well. They practiced making change for a dollar in many ways. Depending on their math skills, they added columns and gave totals. We worked on cookie manners, being polite to customers and writing thank-you notes to those who donated to the Cookie Share.

When it came time for the cookies to be delivered, the girls took the responsibility seriously, delivering boxes and gathering checks. They were thrilled to get their incentives, prizes from the Girl Scouts such as necklaces, tote bags, and pencils, based on how many boxes were sold. All the girls participating got a special badge, and a few in our troop, who sold more than one hundred boxes, also received an extra badge. They took real pride in earning money. For us leaders, we were happy to start building our troop "bank" to take some financial pressure off the parents. At the beginning we disliked having to frequently ask for more money for art supplies, outings, and other activities. It's ideal to have a financially self-sufficient little operation, and even better as the girls are more and more making their own decisions on how that money should be spent.

You could see a little glimmer of each of them as adults, going into graphic design, public relations, accounting, marketing, fund-raising, sales, or event planning as they got into the groove. It's also fun to see the parents, many of whom sold cookies as Girl Scouts when they were kids, encourage their girls.

As they grow older, the girls will become increasingly involved in budgeting and planning for the cookie sale. They can also earn personal finance badges that are particularly geared for ages five through thirteen. From the first year, we encouraged our girls to set goals for themselves that when met were rewarded with fun activities. They get that it's less about the cookie than the experience. But they still love the cookie, too.

Someday, they will likely work to make a living and take care of themselves and their families. They'll probably have bank accounts and trade stocks and think about retirement accounts.

Adding and subtracting the costs and number of boxes ordered are the beginning of real-life math and understanding commerce. At the same time, it's great that they are still little girls who love cookies.

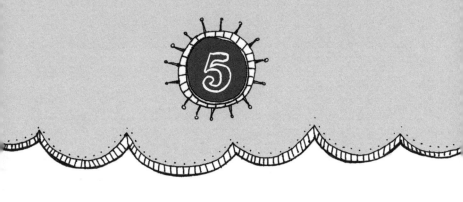

become good at something

"Badges mean nothing in themselves, but they mark a certain achievement and they are a link between the rich and the poor. For if one girl sees a badge on a sister Scout's arm, if that girl has won the same badge, it at once awakens an interest and sympathy between them."

— Daisy in a 1924 speech given at Mercer College, Macon, Georgia

Daisy was lost. She was emotionally battered by her husband's abandonment and death. She continued to travel the world, to immerse herself in painting and sculpting, and to attend many parties. But still, it seemed she felt no real purpose in what she was doing.

One day in May 1911, at a London party, her luncheon partner was Sir Robert Baden-Powell, a celebrated British war hero and founder of the Boy Scouts. It was a seating arrangement—followed by an epiphany—that would change her life.

As they chatted, he told her something bizarre was happening in the Boy Scouts. Girls across the UK were forming their own troops. Then, about six thousand *girls* registered for the Crystal Palace Rally stealthily, using only their initials, and showed up calling themselves Girl Scouts. The girls appeared at the rally wearing homemade uniforms including hats and short skirts. They had heard tales from their brothers and neighborhood boys of building fires, camping out, and taking hikes. The girls not only wanted in, but they wanted their friends in, too. As this was happening, women's roles in American and British society were being challenged, as suffragettes were fighting for the right to vote and more women than ever were working outside the home.

For "B-P," as people called him (or "the B-P"), figuring out what to do about the girls was a problem. He was having enormous success leading the Boy Scouts, where he encouraged them to do one good deed every day and to strive to be responsible and unselfish. B-P's Boy Scout handbook was published in 1908, and by 1911 the group had about forty thousand members. But he had no intention of making Boy Scouts a coed organization. He wanted the groups to be separate and needed a different leader to launch a group for the girls, so he asked his sister Agnes to organize the girls into a sister organization he named "The Girl Guides" in Britain. It seemed serendipitous that Daisy, now a wealthy widow, was at that moment searching for a purpose in life. As Daisy charmed B-P on that day with her passion for art and her storytelling, she listened to him hold forth on the Boy Scouts. He was profoundly influencing the lives of young men. But it was now time to focus on the girls too, and Daisy was happily recruited that day.

As they compared sculpting methods and talked about art instructors, B-P invited Daisy to visit a well-known portrait sculptor together, Signor Lanteri. Afterward, B-P's mother and sister Agnes had tea for Daisy and B-P at their home. Daisy was very interested in palm-reading at the time and took the chance to look at B-P's hands. She wrote in her diary in May of 1911:

> I looked into the lines of his hand, which are very odd and contradictory. The impression he makes on one is equally contradictory. For instance, all of his portraits and all of his writings represent him in action, essentially a man of war, though never has any human given me such a feeling of peace. He rushes from one engagement to another, though he doesn't strike me as restless or pushed or driven. It may be because in his own mind he is not personally seeking anything. His activities are for mankind and he has, perhaps, eliminated the effort to attain things for himself...

Daisy and B-P became close friends, writing numerous letters to each other, sharing thoughts about art and about life. She thought about him often and in June 1911, not long after the luncheon, wrote in her diary: "Today in the few moments I have had to myself, my mind has irresistibly dwelt on B-P. A sort of intuition comes over me that he believes I might make more out of my life, and that he has ideas, which if I follow them, will open a more useful sphere of work before me in the future."

When Daisy told B-P about feeling adrift, he said to her, "There are little stars that guide us on, although we do not realize it," also according to a June 1911 diary entry. Daisy took this advice to heart and counted B-P himself as one of her personal stars. Although in 1912 he married a much younger woman, B-P and Daisy remained very close throughout their lives. Many of their friends thought there was a romantic relationship between the two, and there certainly was a connection, though exactly what it was remains somewhat of a Daisy mystery. Regardless, B-P encouraged Daisy to direct her energy and passion into creating a group for girls. The motto for both Boy Scouts and Girl Scouts, "Be Prepared," shares the initials "B-P," and was something of an inside joke to them. B-P's problem soon became Daisy's obsession.

Soon after, Daisy and B-P happened to be booked on the same ship, the SS *Arcadian* from Southampton, England, to New York together.

There on the outdoor decks and in the dining halls, they talked about plans for introducing scouting to the girls. Many people say that Girl Scouts was brought to America that day when the *Arcadian* landed and Daisy walked off with ideas swimming in her head. This was also the voyage where B-P would meet Olave Soames, his future wife, who was traveling from England to America on the voyage with her father.

STUDIO PORTRAIT OF SIR ROBERT BADEN-POWELL AND JULIETTE GORDON LOW IN UNIFORM, CIRCA 1919.

B-P would continue to encourage Daisy to gather Girl Scouts and form troops. They did not always agree—B-P thought the group should be called Girl Guides as to differentiate the two, and Daisy preferred Girl Scouts. But this was a minor blip in the birth of the movement, and B-P resisted telling Daisy exactly how she should do things. From the beginning, Girl Scouts would be infused with Daisy's own personality and vision. As the Girl Scout organization encouraged girls to become good at something, Daisy found her particular talent. Daisy was good at inspiring the girls.

While the spirit of Girl Scouts has stayed true, the mission statement has changed over the years. In 1946 Girl Scouts changed the statement to: "The purpose of the organization is to help girls realize the ideals of womanhood as a preparation for their responsibilities in the home and as active citizens in the community and in the world." In 1957, the mission was described as: "The purpose of Girl Scouting is to inspire girls with the highest ideals of character, conduct, patriotism, and service that they may become happy and resourceful citizens."

The current mission statement is so far the clearest and simplest, though it may sometime change again: "Girl Scouting builds girls of courage, confidence, and character who make the world a better place."

The World Association of Girl Guides and Girl

Scouts (WAGGGS) established in 1928 in London, England, has ten million members in 145 countries around the world.

Part of the goal of Girl Scouting and Girl Guiding has always been to develop and foster international sisterhood. There are four world centers that offer training, activities, and lodging for girls:

- Our Chalet, Adelboden, Switzerland, opened in 1932
- Pax Lodge (part of the Olave Centre), Hampstead, London, England, opened in 1990
- Our Cabana, Cuernavaca, Mexico, opened in 1957
- Sangam, Pune, India, opened in 1966

When we ask our troop members what their favorite part of Girl Scouts is, or when they speak to other new groups getting started, the girls usually say earning badges is the best part of all. Like Daisy said, it's not badges for badges' sake. But the symbolism and pride of earning a badge, showing that you have worked to make the world a better place—especially for the younger kids—is huge. Our Girl Scout Brownie's have brown sashes that start out with just their troop number and council name, and then gradually become a landscape of little triangles that show their accomplishments. They've earned sports badges for athletic activities, caring and sharing badges for volunteer work, and many more for other pursuits. The badges show that the girls—in some particular way—have become good at that subject or aspect of life. Of course, their expertise varies, but the badges also give them a chance to want to go back and learn more about painting or cooking or how to take care of animals. When we hand the girls a new badge they've earned (usually, simply, in a plastic bag with their name on it), and tell them they did a great job, they guard that bag with their lives. It's a "You go, girl" to wear. Whether we remember back to being kids or even think about our daily lives at work or being a parent, a little encouragement can go for miles and miles. Just like the girls, there are some activities I find more interesting or easier or more challenging than others. I love the craft projects and need to push myself to be better at checking the cookie totals. Together with the girls I was proud of myself for getting up on ice skates after not skating for a while. As a troop we've found a rhythm of activities and projects we really love, many of which the girls are very good at. Those that are new or difficult are in some ways more satisfying when accomplished.

In keeping with the spirit of supporting individuality and embracing one's own interests, girls are also able to create and complete a "Make Your Own Badge." To do this, girls work with their troop leader or other volunteer to invent a badge; they name it, decide what activities need to be done to earn it, and design and produce it. Girl Scouts has suggested badge-making companies who can make the actual badge. But the badge itself is original to the girl, and only the girl, or group of girls, who has created it start to finish can earn it.

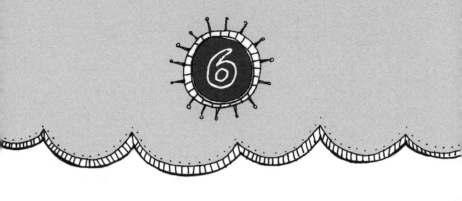

be a sister

"Truly, ours is a circle of friendships, united by our ideals."

—Daisy, 1925

In the summer of 1911 at age fifty, just a few months after meeting B-P, Daisy invited a group of local Scottish girls to Lochs, the castle in Scotland she was renting for the summer. B-P had already visited her there for a few days. With his encouragement, she began to figure out what to do about the girls. Seven girls came to that first meeting, where they ate strawberries and scones and drank tea. One of the girls had walked seven miles to get to Lochs. The group, which included many poor girls from the town, began to meet every Saturday at the castle, where Daisy brought in teachers for such diverse life lessons as knot-tying, map-reading, wool-spinning, and chicken-raising. They had loads of fun, and were also learning practical skills that could help them earn a living. These children already had jobs, as they had to earn money to contribute to their families, but this new knowledge might add to their abilities or aid them in finding better work. The girls themselves became good friends.

After launching groups in Scotland and

England, Daisy returned to Savannah, where she started the first American Girl Scout group. "Come right over! I've got something for the girls of Savannah, and all America, and all the world, and we're going to start it tonight!" said Daisy in a telephone call in 1912 to her cousin Nina Anderson Pape, who ran a local school for girls. That first meeting of eighteen girls in the United States took place on March 12, 1912, at the Louisa S. Porter Home, and is considered the day when the Girl Scouts of the USA was founded. Two groups, or "patrols," were created: the White Rose Patrol and the Carnation Patrol. Daisy registered her niece Margaret "Daisy Doots" Gordon (who was nicknamed after her) as the first official Girl Scout, even though the young girl could not go to the meeting that day. Daisy made plans to turn her carriage house into a new headquarters. It would not have an office feel, but more of a clubhouse. The girls met new friends that day, registered as the first official Girl Scouts, and then told other friends about the new club. In about a month, more than one hundred girls were registered as Girl Scout members.

It turned out Daisy was a natural at gathering Girl Scouts and encouraging them in a fun way—a way that made them want to keep coming back year after year. She became president of the organization in all ways—raising money, developing a vision, engaging experts to adapt the English materials for an American handbook, and recruiting members. She was involved in all aspects, from choosing the colors of the uniform to representing Girl Scouts in other countries around the world. She was enormously proud of what she was creating and delighted in measuring the growth she could see happening every day. In an October 1916 letter, Daisy wrote to her sister Mabel: "To let you realize how my Girl Scout movement is flourishing I must tell you that the receipts in September for that month were $800.00 and that my handbook published in August is almost sold out[.] 4,500 copies sold in two months!"

In the carriage house of Daisy's home, a sign read: "Girl Guide Headquarters," and the girls wore handmade dark blue uniforms with black hair ribbons. They went on many hikes, played sports, and began to earn badges (which had to be hand embroidered) for knowing what to do in a fire, how to make a bed, the history of the U.S. flag, and of course, how to tie several knots. A badge would represent proficiency in a skill or subject and was only given after a specific list of requirements were met. For example, to earn a cyclist badge, a girl would have to own her own bicycle, know how to mend a tire, agree to give the bicycle to the government if needed, and read a map well. Unlike other clubs which focused on one type of sport or activity, Girl Scouts had something for all girls. It was also a place where all girls were welcome.

The Girl Scout Law, which girls recite at meetings, has always had a version of this promise in the final line: "Be a sister to every Girl Scout." For many of us in Girl Scouts, sisterhood is the soul of the Girl Scouts, its fundamental reason for being. Daisy found that as she brought girls together, they became stronger, not only as teams but as individuals. While the girls were to be friends to everyone, their relationship with other Girl Scouts—as sisters—would become a special bond.

The adult women and men who would shape and run the Girl Scout organization over the early years were friends and confidantes of Daisy's, including her goddaughter Anne Hyde Clarke Choate and Lou Henry Hoover, who would later become First Lady of the United States as wife of president Herbert Hoover. The board of directors acted as top donors, advisers, and supporters.

They were, mostly, smart and sophisticated. Many were wealthy. Some of the women officers had not worked outside their homes before to such an extent, and the draw of changing the world for girls became fulfilling work for them. Daisy herself supported Girl Scouts with any money she had, and kept a hand in most every decision or project.

Just a month after the first U.S. Girl Scout meeting, a huge tragedy struck that deeply affected Daisy and her circle of friends. The RMS *Titanic* sank in April 1912, killing more than 1,500 people, including John Jacob Astor IV, then the richest man in the world, and Arthur Ryerson, CEO of Ryerson Steel Company and an old friend of Daisy's. It was a profound personal shock to Daisy, who had become accustomed to traveling back and forth regularly from the U.S. to Great Britain by luxury steamer. In fact, Daisy sailed on the RMS *Baltic*, another White Star Line ship, just a few weeks after the sinking of the *Titanic*.

In May 1912, while on board the *Baltic*, Daisy wrote to her parents about the crew members who did not make it out in time, and about Ryerson's daughters, who not only survived, but also saved other passengers:

...both girls had to row & bail out the boat, because only one able seaman was aboard their life boat[.] Susanne, who is as strong as a man, threw off her fur coat & got into the icy water to help boost up one man who was too cold to get in. They saved 19 men & two died after they got them in their life boat. I look into the familiar faces of these stewards & seamen & I think of all the noble souls who met their death so bravely. It brings forcibly to ones mind the dreadful tragedy.

The *Titanic* disaster had a huge impact on American society, and Daisy personally. But it did not keep her from traveling or from her new goal of making a difference in the lives of girls.

She had recently announced to her family that she'd found something worth doing. She wrote home to her parents in an August 1911 letter: "I like girls, I like this organization and the rules and pastimes, so if you find that I get very deeply interested you must not be surprised!"

Daisy was from a family of six children and had three sisters growing up, Eleanor, Mabel, and Alice. They lived in a big house on Oglethorpe Avenue in Savannah, where they would play in a lush garden and climb in a tall tree. Daisy attended boarding school with both Eleanor and Alice. Because

Mabel was so much younger—twelve years—than Daisy, they had almost a mother-daughter relationship, where Daisy would act as the protector and adviser, especially after Alice died. Mabel remained one of Daisy's closest allies, and the two were prolific letter-writers to each other over many years and across continents.

At Edge Hill Boarding School, Daisy made such good friends that she became sad at the thought of not seeing them at the end of her term. According to her niece, Daisy Gordon Lawrence ("Juliette Gordon School Days"), Daisy wrote in a letter home:

My happy, happy year at Edge Hill is over. All the girls have gone and as I look back on it I wonder how any mortal could manage to squeeze so much pleasure in so short a space of time. I can hardly realize that I will never see some of the girls again, school girl love is called sirlly [silly], but I feal [feel] that in all my after life, I can never love as warmly and purely as I do now. Oh, it seems too sad as soon as I get fond of people, they have to leave me, but there is one comfort in thinking that God or you will never leave me nor forsake me. Please don't laugh at this, I feel so dreadfully lonely.

Daisy enjoyed traveling with her friends and family members, and learning about other countries and cultures firsthand. In 1907 and 1908, Daisy traveled the world, including France, Italy, and India, with her niece, Beth Parker, and Grace Carter, the daughter of a good friend, along with a maid to take care of them. During that time she wrote a detailed diary about the people she met and her international adventures as a favorite aunt-friend taking the young women on a world tour.

Daisy's two closest friends from her New York finishing school, Mary Gale Clarke and Abby Lippitt, were her dearest friends for many years, through happy milestones and life disappointments. Daisy wrote to Mary in 1923: "Your most welcome letter reached me and it did bring back old times! When we three, you, Abby and I were such friends and it seems very wonderful that when thirty-seven years have passed since we three were girls together at old Charbonnier's—yet we still love each other and our friendship stands firm..." Daisy greatly valued her relationships with her close friends and confidantes, including her own sisters, who would eventually help her and stand by her through her failed marriage and then the success of starting the Girl Scouts. Daisy found that it was vital to have her friends around, both in good and bad times.

Daisy believed her Girl Scouts were learning not only to be leaders but to support each other as they grew older. In her poem "A Call," Daisy wrote:

JULIETTE GORDON LOW PRESENTS THE "FOUNDER'S BANNER" TO THE TROOP THAT YEAR WHICH BEST UPHELD THE IDEAS OF THE GIRL SCOUTS ORGANIZATION THE PREVIOUS YEAR. PHOTO TAKEN IN SAVANNAH, GEORGIA, MARCH 24, 1925, WITH THE GIRL SCOUT TROOP FROM THE EPISCOPAL HOME FOR GIRLS IN SAVANNAH, GEORGIA.

"Boy Scouts are trained in the way they should go, but 'tis girls who will count in the next generation."

B-P agreed, writing to Daisy in January 1917 that of the two movements, for boys and girls, the Girl Scouts "…is if anything the more important, since it deals with the mothers of the future who will influence future generations."

And it is true that women's friendships are a common thread holding together the lives of women in every generation. Women are not always born with sisters, but somehow, we find them. We search them out in schools, our neighborhoods and work, because we hope they will reflect us and help us along in our journeys. We form book clubs and running groups and meet each other for coffee not because we want to fill up our calendar, but because we thrive emotionally and physically through time spent with our friends. Women have an undeniable need to be together, to talk about our lives and ease our troubles through humor.

A recent study found that this feeling—that women need to talk to each other and be together—is a scientific fact. Laura Cousino Klein, a professor at Pennsylvania State University and the author of the study, says that when the stress hormone oxytocin is released in a woman, it encourages her to gather with other women and to take care of their children. When she does, more oxytocin is released, which

GIRL SCOUT HEADQUARTERS EARLY STATISTICS

From June 1, 1913, to Jan. 1, 1914

Recorded by Edith D. Johnston, National Secretary

Letters
* Received: 575
* Written: 588

Telegrams
* Received: 11
* Sent: 12

Telephones (From Oct. 1st)
* Received: 28
* Sent: 70

Callers: (From Oct. 1st): 39
* Visits: 10
* Meetings Attended: 1

Handbooks
* Sold: 104
* Complimentary Copies: 48

Badges Sold
* Tenderfoot: 104
* Second Class: 77
* Proficiency: 15
* Troop Crests: 11
* Total: 207

Letters of inquiry regarding movement: 85

Organization:
* No. Cities: 15
* No. Troops: 35
* No. Officers: 31
* No. Scouts: 565

produces a calming feeling. It's called the "tend and befriend" response, and Klein says it helps explain why women generally outlive men, who are more likely to isolate themselves when under stress. Having friends is so vital to a woman's health, found another study by Harvard Medical School, that not having confidants was considered a risk factor akin to smoking or being overweight. Our sisters and sister friends are part of literary history, from *Little Women* to *Pride and Prejudice* to *The Girls from Ames.*

While there is something powerful in a sister by our side, there is also something powerful in a sister who betrays us. Women, and girls, can be meaner to each other than they would ever be to men. Rachel Simmons, author of *Odd Girl Out* and *The Curse of the Good Girl*, has become a leading voice about why girls act this way and what parents can do to stop it. Simmons teaches many of the same beliefs as do Girl Scout leaders, and makes the great point that it is more important to be an authentic girl than a good girl who tries to be perfect but is not being herself. Simmons believes in breaking the curse of the good girl by helping girls understand they don't need to please everyone. Simmons had found in her research that being "nice" all the time on the surface led to hidden feelings that would later emerge as aggression—the mean girl syndrome. In 2000, Simmons founded the nonprofit Girls Leadership Institute in order to bring groups of girls together to teach them skills that help them work through conflicts and problems at their schools.

I had the experience of attending an all-girls Catholic high school, Connelly School of the Holy Child in Potomac, Maryland. Some of my closest friends today I met during my teenage years at that school. One of my high school best friends, Alison Bermack, and I were each other's maids of honor. We also started a website together, *Cooking with Friends*, which encourages people to cook with others rather than alone. What I took with me from Holy Child to college, and then into the real world, was a sense of confidence that girls can do anything. Girls were captains of the soccer team, editors of the yearbook, stars and directors in the school play. I saw girls in every leadership position as a completely natural progression of what we would become. While I'm sure I didn't walk the halls then thinking what an inspiring place it was, I realize it now. Part of that impact came personally from the founder of the Holy Child schools, Cornelia Connelly (1809–1879), who, like Daisy, encouraged girls to be independent and to give service to others.

As a Girl Scout troop leader, I need to go no further than our own meetings to feel the sisterhood spark when our twelve girls stand in a circle, holding hands, right arm over left, singing a song about friendships called "Make New Friends." One girl starts the "squeeze," and it is then passed around the circle to show how their friendship never ends. Yes, those girls might be on the playground not letting one girl into a game a few minutes later. But I believe the circle makes them a little less likely to do that, especially to one of their sisters. These girls began meeting together when they were five or six years old, in kindergarten. Now they're entering third grade. As they choose various after-school activities and inevitably end up in different classrooms, the continuity of their time together as a troop is so valuable. They sometimes surprise us with their love for each other, which they show through waiting their turn for the best scissors when making an art project, not bragging about selling the most cookies, and listening when another girl has something she really wants to say.

It's not easy. We once made a project of Valentine's Day vases for their parents, glued tissue paper in red and pink with little hearts that shone through like stained glass. We brought in jars and bottles of all shapes and sizes. Not everyone could get their favorite. There were tears and major disappointment. But when the last gobs of glue were wiped up, twelve vases, beautiful in a dozen different ways, were arranged on the table. No one said, "I learned a lot from that," but the next time it came to choose different patterns for making a pillow, the girls showed new patience. I wish I could bottle up that inner strength they are learning from each other and drop it onto their foreheads when someone tells them they aren't good enough. But I realize they're forming their own stockpiles of strength inside, to use when they choose, themselves, in their own ways.

I sometimes wonder if they will be friends for life. Some of them may be. But they will all have this common experience at this part of their young childhood, and I feel lucky to be part of it. At our Girl Scout community's annual overnight camping trip, it's thrilling to see the big girls, up through high school, still hanging out together, teaching the little girls, singing "Soul Sister" by the camp-fire, and putting on plays that take teamwork and literary sensibility. I know many of them are going through adolescent angst, issues with the way they look and what they eat, and changing relationships with boys. But they know they have friends.

One spring day we played a game of "What if?" as part of earning the Caring and Sharing badge. "What do you do if...your best friend is crying?"

was the first question. Many hands shot up. I love hearing their voices, the way they describe their feelings and thoughts in their own words and patterns. "I ask her what's wrong." "I find a teacher or grown-up." "Sometimes things get tough and confusing, and I tell her I cry too." Empathy filled the room as those who weren't talking listened intently. Next, "What do you do if…one of the girls in your troop has a birthday?" "Sing happy birthday!" "Be really nice to her all day." "Make her a card, with pictures." "Surprise her with something she didn't know about." And, "What do you do if…your mother has to finish a big project for work the next day?" "Take care of my little sister so she doesn't bug her." "Ask her how I can help." "Work on the project with her." "Do my homework and read so she can think better."

This kind of interaction is why Girl Scouts works. You can tell a girl to be nice and think of others' feelings, but if she talks about it, thinks about it, and acts it out with other girls, it's much more likely to become second nature to her.

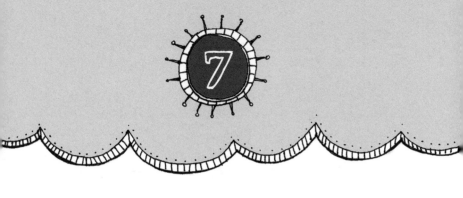

challenge yourself

"Welcome all obstacles, as it is only by meeting with difficulties that you can know how to overcome them and Be Prepared for others in the future..."

—How Girls Can Help Their Country,
Handbook for Girl Scouts (1913)

When Daisy was in her twenties, she had a terrible pain in her ear. She insisted her doctor treat the ear infection with what she thought was the newest and best cure, silver nitrate, a natural antiseptic. The doctor was not familiar with the treatment and did not want to try it, but Daisy eventually prevailed. It was a devastating disaster. Not only did the silver nitrate fail to work, but the treatment caused partial deafness.

Several years later, as wedding guests threw rice at Daisy and Billow after their beautiful ceremony, a grain of rice became lodged in Daisy's good ear. A few days into the honeymoon on St. Catherine's Island in Georgia, the couple rushed back to Savannah to have Daisy's ear examined. When the doctor tried to remove the rice, he punctured her ear drum and damaged the nerves, making her completely deaf in that ear.

The degree of Daisy's deafness could change based on individual circumstances, like weather, humidity, and how rested she was. She certainly used deafness to her advantage when she wanted to, especially when someone said no to a request to volunteer for or donate to the Girl Scouts. If someone declined, Daisy would smile and effusively thank her for the generous offering of money or time. But other times it was clear that she couldn't hear a thing. She never let deafness slow her down though, and lived life to its fullest, traveling, going to parties, and having discussions with everyone she met. She did use the most modern hearing aids, although sometimes she turned them down or off. Sometimes, the hearing aid would emit a loud feedback and others around her would advise her to adjust the volume.

JULIETTE GORDON LOW, CIRCA 1890.

Many people probably noticed that she did more talking than listening, and that she loved to tell stories. She became known as a great storyteller, particularly of ghost stories around the campfire and tales of her own youth.

In her work and in her regular life, Daisy tried to not let her deafness get in the way. But she did find that it caused miscommunication, sometimes with comic effect. During one Girl Guide event in London, Daisy thought it was incredibly rude that the audience was not clapping for the speaker. So each time the speaker paused, Daisy clapped loudly and hooted. She later found out that the speech was in honor of her, so as the woman said things like "Daisy Low is so wonderful," Daisy was cheering for herself.

It was remarkable how much Daisy accomplished while not being able to hear. One of Daisy's many favorite stories was about the time she was walking in Scotland near an overflowing stream. She had stopped along the way at a log she would need to use to cross over. Just then, a peddler came up, and she instantly prevailed upon him to help her across as she could not hear well. She insisted he start ahead of her with her following and holding onto his shoulder. The peddler tried to object,

JULIETTE GORDON LOW CIRCA 1889, SAVANNAH, GEORGIA.

but Daisy would not respond to his pleas. When they had crossed to the other side, she thanked him and asked finally what he was trying to tell her. He replied that he was simply attempting to say...he was blind.

While she didn't like to bring attention to her deafness, it gave Daisy a strong position to argue for equality and inclusivity among the Girl Scouts, and she made sure that girls with disabilities, as well as girls from diverse racial, economic, and religious backgrounds were welcome. Activities and excursions were to be kept low-cost or paid for by troop funds, to make sure all girls could participate. Daisy criticized another group of girls she felt were geared toward the elite, and in fund-raising letters would point out that Girl Scouts would be a place for both the wealthy and underprivileged and for minorities as well.

The first African American Girl Scout troop was formed in 1917. By the 1920s there were African American troops in cities all over the country, including Boston, Indianapolis, Nashville, New York, and Philadelphia. Then, in the 1950s, the Girl Scouts began an effort to include all races in troops, rather than separating them. In 1956, Martin Luther King Jr. recognized the power of the Girl Scout movement, calling it "a force for desegregation." Daisy trained Josephine Holloway, the first African American Girl Scout staff member, herself.

One of the biggest ongoing controversies about Girl Scouts was whether it was religious enough or too religious. It seems strange now that Daisy would have to do this, but from the early days she fielded criticism from some religious groups that Girl Scouts encouraged girls to be too independent, too athletic, and too interested in a career. In ensuing years, Girl Scouts has been criticized for both being too religious and not religious enough.

Daisy was an Episcopalian, and she was personally very spiritual. She prayed as a regular part of her life, and kept a Bible given to her by her mother when she went away to boarding school, a prized possession that she would often read and quote from. When her brother George Arthur Gordon asked Daisy why she decided to transport the iron gates she had made from England to Savannah (which were quite heavy and expensive to ship), she said, "When I get depressed, or doubtful about what I should do, I shut my eyes, open the bible, and put my finger on a verse. I often get excellent council. [sic]" Gordon relayed this discussion in an April 1935 speech at a Girl Scout conference in Richmond, Va. Apparently, on this day, her finger landed on the last words in the Book of Proverbs: "And let her own works praise her in the gates." Daisy took that to mean her work of art should be at her family home. As Daisy could be deeply religious, at the same time, she was also fascinated by the mystical world. She had her horoscope read and documented, liked reading palms, and was interested by supernatural stories.

But when it came to Girl Scouts, Daisy was highly conscious of religious inclusivity and believed that girls should learn religion at home rather than from their troop leaders. In a 1920 letter, Daisy wrote to a Miss Howells: "We meet all sects on common ground and encourage every child to follow faithfully the faith of its parents, this wise provision was made by Sir Robert Baden-Powell when he began this great work for Boys and Girls." The Girl Scout Promise mentions God, but in 1993 the Girl Scout organization announced that if they wanted to, girls could substitute a name from their own faith tradition. The Girl Scouts as a group do not accept discrimination of any kind, including that of sexual orientation or preference. The key is to support the girl the way she is, rather than turning her into something she is not.

In 1924, Daisy sent letters to the Girl Scouts who had achieved the Golden Eaglet, the highest honor for Girl Scouts. The question had come up whether girls with a handicap or physical disability should be able to win the Golden Eaglet award. Daisy asked the girls in her letter whether they thought a handicapped girl should be able to win the award, even if she might not physically be able to meet some of the requirements, such as swimming or running. Daisy makes no secret of her opinion, writing in the letter: "It has been said that the public will expect to find in our Golden Eaglets perfect specimens of Girlhood, mentally, morally and physically, but may I suggest that our greatest need and the most important thing is that we present to the world and to the Girl Scouts themselves, a perfect example of the SPIRIT OF SCOUTING and that spirit is shown, when one of these afflicted ones by heroic efforts, overcomes difficulties and achieves success in spite of her handicap." Daisy clearly thought a favorable vote would help not just the individual girl, but the group as a whole: "We cannot afford to lose the inspiration that these girls give to their sister Scouts, or the influence they wield in leading others to soar above difficulties."

This was hardly the first or only time Daisy asked the girls what they thought. Daisy adamantly made sure that Girl Scouts was not entirely driven by the grown-up leaders and parents of the girls. From the beginning, when a difficult question came up she would say, "Let's ask the girls."

In a 1952 written remembrance, one of Daisy's friends and Girl Scout coworkers, Dorris Hough, recalls her saying, "The Angel Gabriel couldn't make them take anything they don't like," about misguided efforts to convince the girls to think a certain way. At one Girl Scout convention, Hough remembers a group of leaders proposing that badges be replaced by small black hatch marks, which would make the uniforms look neater than the jumble of various sized and colored badges. "No," said Daisy. "In the first place that's a grown up's idea, the girls wouldn't like it all. Second, the badges show what a girl is proficient in—how could you tell from a black line whether she could cook or swim? And third, you couldn't copyright a black line nor sell it."

For the Girl Scouts as an organization, the biggest challenge over the years has been how to stay current and how to keep the girls' interest as they are constantly offered new activities and things to do with their after-school and week-end time. If Girl Scouts has lost anything by not jumping on the latest fads or trying to become edgy, it has gained it back by steadfastly keeping the focus on the girls and staying true to its spirit. Between 2004 and 2005, Girl Scouts took a critical look at itself, Michelle Tompkins, Girl Scout spokeswoman told me. The group decided to try to make the Girl Scout experience more consistent from council to council, beginning with cutting the number of councils across the U.S. from 313 to 112. They worked on modernizing the logo because the girls said, "The green looks like it's been in the sun a little too long." Some things have not changed, however. "We ask the girls what they want," says Tompkins. "We back them up."

As troop leaders and also as parents, one of our biggest challenges is to let the girls do more for themselves. It sounds simple, but especially for the littlest ones, we are conscious of their safety, their feelings, and the need to move things along in meetings and for events to finish on time. But when we relax a bit and open the door to let the girls choose the activity, to lead their own discussion, or to vote on a new way of doing things, we are each time reminded that they are in the Girl Scouts to learn independence and to practice it. Sometimes we have to be patient, but these are the times when the girls say and do the most amazing things. This is also when we learn the most from them. While there are rules and traditions in Girl Scouts that the girls love and appreciate for their familiarity and the way they make things work, there is in each group plenty of room to develop a troop culture based on kids' interests.

Our first year, as new leaders, Melissa and Sherry and I started noticing how the girls really flourished and became more confident and creative when we gave them just a little bit of independence in choosing a game or activity, or even asked their opinions. If they weren't paying attention, they would wake up. If they were sitting waiting for an activity to be placed in front of them, they would get up and move more, making their own decisions. Like so many other things about Girl Scouts, we then realized what we were doing had a name: "Girl-Led." The next stage is "Girl Scouts' Own." This is a girl-planned activity or series of songs, poems, or programs that helps them express what they are feeling. When they're really little, we've found giving them choices, say three options for the next badge to work on, or two choices for a banner theme, work well. They like voting and they like having their voices heard as they work to come to a consensus on something.

When we had a meeting at Christmas and Hanukah time, we asked the girls to start a discussion about their own holiday traditions—the food, the music, and who comes to visit—instead of us telling them what holidays are all about. A face-painting party meant the girls would paint each other—maybe it turned out messier, but it was creative, and it was theirs.

It has been amazing to see the older girls, middle school and above, jump forward in that independence by planning meetings for the younger ones. The "big girls" in our area help plan encampment, our annual overnight camping trip, from the games to the meals to the campfire storytelling. One middle school group came in to teach our little ones songs that we would all then sing together at a big camp-out. They taught our girls how to sing in rounds, and their voices were beautiful and clear as they stood before us singing:

White coral bells upon a slender stalk
Lilies of the Valley deck my garden walk
Oh, don't you wish
That you could hear them ring?
That will happen only when the fairies sing.

Because we work on so many different activities—art to sports to nature—it has also been interesting to see girls find things they excel in, and to have that feeling and true understanding of being "good at" something. It's okay if they're not all great at everything. Part of the power of Girl Scouts is not focusing on only one thing or ability. At the same time, the girls challenge themselves in the other activities that might not come as naturally. What's really remarkable is that the girls figure these things out on their own, and then shift into roles as teacher and student to help each other. They are also doing groundwork in individual responsibility. One year, after an early meeting, the teacher whose classroom we borrowed after school for meetings politely let us know that we left it considerably dirtier than it was before. We were embarrassed and at the next meeting made good use of our "kaper" chart where girls are each assigned a duty: taking attendance, craft cleanup, snack setup, and more. We talked with the girls about the importance leaving a borrowed space better than we found it.

As second graders, our girls helped another "sister" troop get started. We knew of ten or more girls who wanted to join our troop, but felt that ours had reached an ideal group size of twelve. A whole new group should be started, we understood, but we were having a hard time finding someone to lead the group. Our Girl Scouts of Wisconsin Badgerland Council membership specialist, Laura, held a meeting at our kids' school to introduce the parents. Melissa and Sherry and I spoke about why we became volunteers. Part of it is that we get to spend more time with our own kids. We emphasized how much genuine fun we have getting to know these girls better, watching them grow, and seeing their friendships with each other become stronger.

A grandmother of one of the girls, who had been her own daughter's troop leader, stepped forward to volunteer, as did several other parents. There were many volunteer options—leading one meeting, teaching an activity, or chaperoning an event. Our troop came to the new group's first organizational meeting, in the art room of the school. While the parents talked and filled out paperwork, our girls had the new girls form a circle. They recited the Promise, the Girl Scout Law, and sang "Make New Friends,"

Make new friends, but keep the old.
One is silver, and the other gold.

A circle's round; it has no end.

That's how long I want to be your friend.

And "The Brownie Smile Song" (words and music by Harriet F. Heywood):

I have something in my pocket

That belongs across my face.

I keep it very close to me

In a most convenient place.

I bet you'll never guess it

If you guessed a long, long while.

So, I'll take it out and put it on;

It's a great big Brownie smile!

This concept of challenging yourself—even risking failure by trying something new—is a key part of success in so many parts of our lives. In the technology industry, which I covered as a journalist for more than a decade, I saw the smartest engineers, venture capitalists, and marketers dare to make mistakes and even to fail. They tried wild ideas that everyone said wouldn't work. They were terrified of losing money, customers, market share, or reputation. Many did fail, which gave them greater knowledge for the next try. A few made incredible things happen. Some may have found success through luck, but more made their own luck by being ready for a moment when it came. Combine a little fear and hard work, and confidence will happen, whether you are a CEO or a kid.

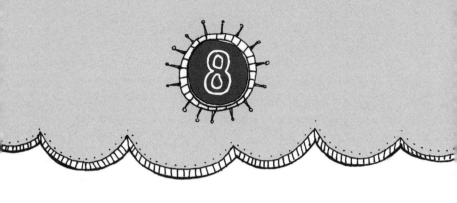

knowledge and understanding are empowering

"Girl Scouting is not just knowing...but doing...
not just doing, but being."

—The Girl Scout Handbook, 1956

As Daisy set out to publish a first Girl Scout guidebook at her home in Savannah, a large problem loomed. There was no money to print the book, and Daisy refused to ask "the girls" for any financial help. Instead, she would decorate her hat with carrots, parsley, and other garden vegetables, slightly past their prime as to look more downtrodden, and wear it to society lunches. When people asked her about the hat, she'd say, sadly, her Girl Scouts sorely needed money and she was saving anything she could for them, so of course she had to trim her hat with garden scraps rather than buying a new one. As the women looked at her, shocked, Daisy used that opportunity to ask if they, too, would like to support the Girl Scouts through a donation or volunteer work.

Daisy would continue to be creative with her fund-raising. A few years later, in 1915, when she needed money for operating expenses, Daisy sold her pearls. Girl Scouts national treasurer Ted Coy paid $2,800 for the necklace as a Christmas gift for his wife.

The creation of a Girl Scout handbook would be an important step forward for the organization, and it had been a milestone for the Boy Scouts

PORTRAIT OF JULIETTE GORDON LOW BY MOFFETT STUDIO, 1920S.

as well. *How Girls Can Help Their Country* was first published in 1913. Much of it was adapted from *How Girls Can Help to Build Up the Empire,* by B-P's sister Agnes Smyth Baden-Powell, but Daisy and B-P both believed the girls and boys should each have their own specific handbooks, as should the British and American girls. Daisy recruited noted naturalist Walter J. Hoxie to lead the girls on outdoor expeditions, be the caretaker at the Camp Lowlands, train girls and leaders, and write the new handbook. Hoxie particularly excelled at his nature advice, which can be seen in a line about the importance of planting trees: "A tree is a tree anyway be it large or small... There are no bad trees." Later editions, in 1916 and 1917, were spearheaded by Daisy.

There is much practical advice in the first handbook about physical and mental skills needed, not just to be Girl Scouts, but to survive in the world. An elaborate section on knot-tying advises: "As it may happen some day that a life may depend on a knot being properly tied you ought to know the proper way." Reading the early versions of the handbook, it's striking how so many things in our culture have changed, such as Velcro's influence on the importance of knot-tying. But simultaneously, so many things, such as needing exercise and being able to navigate around your neighborhood or city, are much the same.

The publication of the guide was validation in black and white that the Girl Scout movement was here to stay. The guidebook was released at a particularly poignant moment in world history, during World War I, as children searched for ways to help their fathers, brothers, and their country through difficult times. Girls all over the world were trying to find themselves and to be useful to society, which Daisy had finally done herself in founding the Girl Scouts. As echoed by the title, and greatly influenced by B-P's thinking, Daisy felt it was a girl's duty to help her country, in part by becoming a stronger individual.

"It is the aim of this organization to teach girls how to be happy, vigorous, resourceful girls and how to become efficient, self-helpful women," an early promotional Girl Scout publication advised.

A few years later, in 1918, Daisy helped create a silent movie to introduce Girl Scouts to the world, entitled "The Golden Eaglet: The Story of a Girl Scout." The film opens with two girls wandering aimlessly around their town with nothing to do. The girls then discover the Girl Scouts, with their fun activities of camping, swimming, and hiking. The story turns to focus on one girl, Margaret, who, in true Girl Scout spirit, swims across a lake in her clothes and hat, saves a man who has been hit on the head by a robber, and then takes over the care of a family whose father is a soldier away at war and whose mother is working all day in the factory. Margaret and the other Girl Scouts tend to a sick daughter, scrub a filthy kitchen and a filthier baby, sweep the floors, make the bed, hoe the garden, and then, when the mother comes home to her newly clean and organized house, offer to teach her canning. Of course, Margaret earns the Golden Eaglet award for all of her work. The movie ends by suggesting the viewer start her own troop by contacting the national headquarters. Daisy herself appears in the movie, pinning Margaret with the Golden Eaglet. Daisy is also shown at her desk at the very end of the movie, in her Girl Scout uniform and hat, looking up with a smile.

There are, in *How Girls Can Help Their Country*, many straightforward, useful bits of advice, such as how to make the Girl Scout salute (three fingers straight up with the thumb holding down the pinkie finger), how to clean window screens, cure

JULIETTE GORDON LOW, FOUNDER, GIRL SCOUTS OF THE USA, IN HER OFFICE, CIRCA 1914-1918.

a ham, make a mousetrap, and stop a nose bleed. The girl reading the book would be expected to "Be Prepared" for most anything life could throw her way.

But in addition to the common-sense advice there is thought-provoking philosophy, such as "Have you ever stopped to think that your most constant companion throughout life will be yourself?"; "The influence of women over men is vastly greater than that of men over one another"; and "Try to see everything. Consider it almost a disgrace if, when with others, they see anything big or small, high or low, near or far, that you fail to discover. See it first if you can." It's through these deeper thoughts that girls get a sense of why they are learning these practical skills. Girl Scouting is not just a series of unrelated classes in drawing, knot-tying, or archery, but an inter-related life lesson.

The best Girl Scouts would have certain unde-niable attributes. They were thrifty ("Girl Scouts should never go into debt"), physically fit, got lots of fresh air, and did good things for others. The handbook advises against trying to do two things at once; suggests that frogs are helpful in gardens; and encourages girls to breathe through their noses, never their mouths. Eventually, millions of girls would read these words, and many of them would follow this advice.

Several parts in the book suggest girls focus on choosing one occupation, on becoming very good at a certain trade that will give them independence. "Whatever you take up, do it with all your might, and stick to it," it says. Suggestions include architecture, firefighting, medicine, and aviation. Chemist and physicist Marie Curie is invoked as an example, showing that women can not only succeed in their careers, but become pioneers. It is also suggested that girls master something else as a backup, in case the first career does not work out, and points out that women will likely also have an additional job at home.

The handbook makes frequent reference to "housewifery" and the high probability that at some point, Girl Scouts will need to cook and clean like their mothers and grandmothers. In that vein it advises on household duties in ways to make them more interesting, such as stopping to recognize the beauty of the earth while gardening, and embracing the calmness that can come from needlework. At the same time, it advises on ways to be thrifty. Girls should become self-reliant in their houses, never assuming to count on a husband or maid to take care of everything. The advice is sometimes so specific that it is funny: "Any bad smell in a house is a danger signal; find out its cause, and get rid of it." It is advised that if you want to eat, you should better be able to cook for yourself. Recipe ideas and cooking tips include: "Boiling water is useful to dip your sardine into if you want to get his skin off. But do not dip him into the tea-kettle."

Girls were assured that even the most mundane tasks had deep value. "Needlework is good for all of us," the handbook says. "It rests and calms the mind. You can think peacefully over all the worries of Europe whilst you are stitching. Sewing generally solves all the toughest problems, chiefly other people's."

When Daisy first started the Girl Scouts, some American parents, just like some had in Britain with the Girl Guides, worried how Girl Scouting would affect their girls. Concerns ranged from the fear that girls could become tomboys if they learned things like how to start a campfire and outrace an opponent; how exactly the girls would be chaperoned; what clothing they would wear; and even that the girls would mix with people of other parts of society that were not like them. Some of that concern was assuaged because Daisy's family was so proper and well-regarded. They thought that, while Daisy may have been eccentric, she was still a lady. She clearly liked nice things, but she was also willing to work for them. As it says in an early Girl Scout handbook: "Roughing it is all very fine to talk about, but it is best to make your camp as comfortable as possible."

As for advancing as a Girl Scout, there were specific requirements enumerated to earn badges and to graduate to higher levels in Girl Scouting. A first-class Girl Scout, for example, had to be able to set a table, walk one mile in twenty minutes, have fifty cents in the bank she'd earned herself, and be able to identify and name ten trees and ten birds. Some of the badges that can be earned include Invalid Cooking (to cook for the sick, girls must own a bicycle and learn how to cook gruel), Dairy (must know how to make butter and milk a cow), Marksmanship (must know how to load a pistol, and be proficient in archery), and Pathfinder (must be able to draw a map of her neighborhood and find the points of a compass by the stars or sun).

Part of the goal of *How Girls Can Help Their Country* was to instill confidence in the girls. Those reading this book and learning its lessons, from how to stop runaway horses to how to save someone who has fallen through the ice, surely feel more prepared. And that is what Daisy wanted, not just for herself, but for her girls; to know they have the power and independence to make things happen. "Each one of us has her own destiny in her control, and has her own personal problems in life to settle" (*How Girls Can Help Their Country*, 1916 edition).

As I researched Daisy's life and peeled back the layers about why and how she founded the Girl Scouts, I wanted to bring back some of her story to our own girls. While in Savannah, I bought twelve "Daisy" Brownie patches, so that as these girls went on a history tour during our Madison meetings, they could learn more about Daisy, and earn the badge.

First, I asked the girls to close their eyes. Then, I began an imaginary tour:

Picture the time as 1912, almost one hundred years ago. Women were likely to wear dresses every day, not just for parties or special events. They traveled on boats and trains, rarely on airplanes (though Daisy did go up in airplanes, of course), and it was just becoming popular to own a car; many people still used horse-drawn carriages, or more commonly, walked everywhere. There was no Internet, no cell phones, no microwave ovens, iPods, or e-readers. There was no television, and movies were silent, meaning you could see the actors but not hear their voices. Women were not allowed to vote in elections.

I could see their eyes fluttering a bit, and then settling. I went on:

In Savannah, it is usually much warmer weather than in Madison. There are big oak trees with lots of Spanish moss covering them and hanging from their branches. People talk with southern accents, and they like to eat southern foods like grits, black-eyed peas, and okra.

Then I had them open their eyes. They were quiet, transported. I showed them pictures of Daisy and her family's beautiful house (known as "The Birthplace" in Savannah), and the intricate ironwork gates she created that stand there today. "The Birthplace" is now a museum about Daisy and her life.

I continued:

In many ways it was a completely different time. But Girl Scouts were still much like you. They liked to play games and sports, draw pictures and make crafts, and talk with their friends. They went to school and learned to read and do math. So when Juliette Gordon Low, who everyone called Daisy, invited the first group of girls that year to have tea and strawberries and start the Girl Scouts, they were very excited.

I had been a bit nervous about giving a history lesson to the girls, but I could see in their faces that they were utterly fascinated. Then the questions came: "Who was president when the Girl Scouts were started?"; "Where did she get her clothes?"; and "Did Daisy have children?" It clearly dawned on the girls that what they did in Girl Scout meetings and activities was inspired by this one particular woman. She was important in their lives today, even though she lived many years ago. They were amazed that a historical figure could have such an impact on them. I heard later from some of the parents that their daughters had started to talk about "Daisy" as if they knew her personally, and even as if they would know what she thought about something.

Just like those first eighteen American girls, our girls then sat down to a proper tea. They delighted in pretending they were young ladies from 1912, holding their tea cups carefully and talking in southern accents. Our craft that day was making tea party hats by gluing colorful ribbons and silk flowers onto white floppy bonnets. They looked the part.

Next, we talked about how some of the badges the Girl Scouts earned over the years have changed, and how some are almost exactly the same. They got a kick out of hearing that there used to be badges for learning Morse code, semaphore signaling, and developing photographic film (after I explained what all those things were). Some other early badges included Dairy Maid, Milliner, and Laundress ("show the heights at which you can with the least fatigue, use a laundry tub and ironing board," suggests a 1930 Girl Scout handbook), although the Laundress badge was first introduced in 1913). But many other badges, such as those for swimming, painting, finding stars, and sports, are "evergreen" badges. Girls enjoy earning them now as much as the original Girl Scouts did then. Some early badges that now seem prescient are Electrician, introduced in the 1913 handbook, and Business Woman and Interpreter, named in the 1920 handbook.

One longtime favorite badge is the First Aid badge, and we started by making, stocking, and even decorating (these girls love art projects of any kind) individual first aid kits that the girls

IN 1913 SAVANNAH GIRL SCOUTS WORK ON EARNING THEIR FIRST AID BADGE BY PRACTICING ON NEIGHBORHOOD BOY JOHNNY MERCER, WHO WOULD LATER BECOME THE FAMOUS SONGWRITER, AND WHO WAS NOT ACTUALLY HURT AT THE TIME.

could bring on overnight trips or to school in their backpacks. While they worked on their kits, we told them about the day one of Daisy's first groups learned about first aid, and a big misunderstanding ensued. Daisy's girls spent hours pretending to care for each other's wounds, wrapping heads and arms, bandaging everywhere they could, and laying their "patients" out on stretchers. When the mothers came to pick up their daughters from Girl Scouts, they thought the whole troop had been in some kind of terrible accident, and began fainting and screaming. We decided not to do a modern interpretation of this part of the history.

One of the early Girl Scout troops practiced first aid by finding a (perfectly healthy) neighborhood boy named Johnny Mercer, wrapping him up with bandages, and carrying him around on a stretcher. The boy later became a famous songwriter, writing lyrics for more than fifteen hundred songs. "Moon River," "Come Rain or Come Shine," and "The Shadow of Your Smile" are some of his most famous songs.

At our next meeting as we finished the Daisy history badge, we were lucky to borrow fourteen historical Girl Scout uniforms from our local Girl Scout of Wisconsin Badgerland Council office. At the council, in a tiny closet that is much like a secret half-room, there hang close to one hundred uniforms, of many years, sizes, and designs, most in green and khaki hues. The oldest I found was from 1942, and other interesting ones had a mod-fashion 1970s look. The council gave me free reign in the little room, and I chose a wide variety, some with huge collars or floppy ties, and others with beautifully sewn badges, and more with a mid-century feel. We laid them out on tables and let the girls choose which ones to wear, and then took them on a traveling fashion show around the school as they giggled uncontrollably.

No matter where Daisy traveled around the world, whenever she did she sported her wide-brimmed Girl Scout hat, uniform, and a whistle on a string around her neck. Packs of girls would run up to her, peppering her with questions: "How many girls should be in a troop?"; "What shoes should we wear?"; "How do I tie the reef knot?" Like our girls today, they learned all these things by doing them.

Daisy adored her own uniform. She may have had decades of dressing in the most expensive and beautifully tailored clothes befitting a society woman, but the fashion that interested her most now was that of the Girl Scout uniform. As the Girl Scout uniform officially changed from blue to khaki to green, and in all of its decade-specific incarnations, girls of each time period wore theirs proudly, Daisy most of all. She had finally found herself as a person through Girl Scouts, and the uniform was like a second, familiar skin to her.

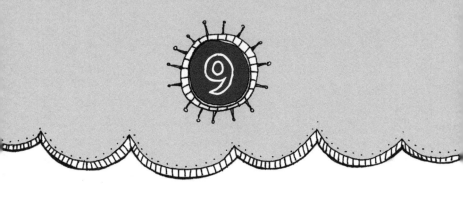

have fun

"I hope that we shall all remember the rules of this Girl Scouting game of ours. They are: To play fair. To play in your place. To play for your side and not for yourself. And as for the score, the best thing in a game is the fun and not the result..."

— Daisy, in a message to Girl Scouts
in the 1924 handbook

As the first Girl Scout headquarters was readied at Daisy's carriage house, she knew the girls must have an outdoor space to play games. One of her top priorities was to create a basketball court. But in those days, it was considered necessary to shield girls playing in just their bloomers (as it was very uncomfortable to play in long dresses, tie-up shoes and underwear were used as athletic wear) from prying eyes. That particular corner at Drayton Street was a busy one, too, with many people walking past all day. So Daisy had a basketball net put up and then hung enormous sheets of canvas all around the outside of the courtyard like curtains, creating a private play space for the girls. They also used the spot for practicing marching, first aid, and other activities. Later, Daisy convinced the city of Savannah to install outside lights around the court, so the girls who worked during the day in factories and in other jobs could come play in the evening. The simple art of play—for girls big and little—was at the core of Daisy's beliefs. Daisy herself had a ritual that every year on her birthday, October 31, she would stand on her head, for fun, and to prove that she could.

THE CARNATION BASKETBALL TEAM, 1914.

Daisy also hired carpenters to convert the interior of the carriage house from a garage to club rooms for activities and enjoyment for the Girl Scouts. There was a little boy of ten years old around during all of this activity, Ogden Nash, who would later become a famous poet, known especially for his humorous rhyming poems. (One of his poems, "Ode to Baby," in its entirety is: "A bit of talcum/is always walcum".) His family was renting the house and carriage house at the time. Daisy offered to reduce the rent as she reclaimed the carriage house, but Nash's father said he would continue to pay the full amount to support the Girl Scouts' launch, thereby becoming one of the first financial supporters of the organization.

As many sorrows and confusions Daisy went through in her life, she continuously managed to pull herself back together again to have fun. She never had any guilt about that. And while she enjoyed leading Girl Scouts and could be very serious about what they needed to know and how they should learn, she also made them understand that if they weren't having fun, well, nothing else really mattered.

Daisy's sense of humor was offbeat and mischievous. But people loved to be around her. One of her young friends, Eleanor Arnett Nash, sister of Ogden Nash, and an early Guide Mistress as they called troop leaders back then, described her this way: "She had a wicked wit, and a charm I am too word-poor to describe. She was quicksilver and pepper—the whole leavened with humanity and laughter. She was the person I most liked to be with."

As much as Daisy was the leader of the Girl Scouts, she always thought of herself as one of the girls, too. In January 1924, she wrote to each girl who had received the Golden Eaglet award, sending a photograph of herself and asking for a picture of them, so they would get to know each other better. "I will know what you look like and I will keep it always," Daisy wrote in the letter.

What is now known as the Girl Scouts' "Founder's Day," is Daisy's birthday, October 31. She loved having a Halloween birthday, with all the dressing up, games and tricks, and eerie stories. "It cheers me to think that the Founder's Day of the Girl Scouts and All Halloween, which brings us so many charming games, are so associated.

JULIETTE GORDON LOW IN UNIFORM AWARDING
GOLDEN EAGLET TO GIRL SCOUT, 1919.

For Girl Scouting is a game too," she wrote in her annual birthday message to Scouts in *The American Girl* magazine in 1924.

In the movie *Whip It*, her directorial debut in 2009, Drew Barrymore embraced the quirky, playful quality of Girl Scouts by naming her all-girl super-empowered roller derby team the "Hurl Scouts." Their uniforms were makeshift versions of the Girl Scout vests and sashes. It was totally in keeping with Girl Scout fun, creative competition, and trying to find out who you are. Barrymore also visited the Birthplace in Savannah in 2009, to the great delight of the many girls who were also there that day and who had their photos taken with her.

Early on as troop leaders, Melissa, Sherry, and I realized that these wonderfully wild kids would go stir-crazy if we didn't move around at every meeting. So we came up with the idea of "the sillies," as in, "shake out the sillies." So, after we form a circle and say the Promise and the Girl Scout Law (we do this at every single meeting—they love the ritual and were so proud when they memorized it on their own), each girl chooses something that we all then do ten times. We chose ten to represent the ten petals on the Daisy flower and the ten parts of the Promise. We've done the following: jump on one leg, turn in a circle, pat your head while rubbing your tummy, stick out your tongue, and cry on the floor like a baby. That last one is my least favorite. It is really, really loud multiplied by twelve. But I really do like the jumping jacks and others that get us up and down and all around—and laughing together right away. Sometimes the girls will bring in a thought from their day, like looking for a leprechaun on St. Patrick's Day—ten times.

We have had meetings on social justice, saving a drowning swimmer, and why we give gifts to others, all profound and important and useful. But just being silly together is one of our best activities; it makes us forget the travails of the day, and we are all equal when we are giggling and jumping around not worrying what anyone thinks of us.

Having fun is probably one of those things best done and not overanalyzed. Play is such a natural part of childhood that it is like air or water. But it is also a key part of how our girls get along with each other and enjoy themselves at our meetings and activities. For us, a huge part of the fun, which grows as the girls get older, are the creative pursuits of art, music, and dance.

Our girls are really in their fun zone when they have paints, markers, crayons, and fabric in front of them. We have made beaded bracelets using the colors of the Daisy petals; decorated backpacks to keep sashes and other Girl Scout treasures in; and even colored individual first aid boxes with names, flowers, and designs. Our macramé day making key chains was lots of fun, and the kids got a kick out of designing their own Halloween treat baskets. When we put out twelve blank backpacks or piles of string, I love seeing how they each tackle the project, and how everyone ends up with different colors, patterns and designs. The girls will often ask me "What's our craft today?" at the beginning of a meeting. I think they thrive on the focused creativity. And they like to show their parents what they did that day.

Every year we take the girls to a holiday season ballet performance of *The Nutcracker*. They love the costumes, the scenery, the gorgeous movement, and beautiful music. But maybe even more, they love to dance with each other. We had a dance party where a hip-hop teacher taught them cool steps, and a Hawaiian luau—in the dead of Wisconsin winter—where they donned leis and colorful skirts and got crazy. It's hard to overestimate the power of communal laughter. When you are laughing with someone, you are sharing a moment, no words or explanation needed.

Fun is a common current through so much of Girl Scouting—being outside, doing art, playing games and sports, and learning something new, all the while developing leadership skills. Even taking risks can be fun, whether you succeed or fail. One of the images I love to think about is our girls bobbing for apples for the first time. We filled a big metal tub with water and threw in some apples. The girls put their hands behind their backs and tried to bite into an apple. It took many tries, getting hair wet, and breaks to let out a peal of laughter and the water drip off their faces. But at the end, each girl succeeded, and took a real chunk out of a cold, delicious, sweet apple, a well-deserved reward for playing the game.

be outdoors

"It is in the open, where they learn woodcraft and nature lore, that a girl gets the best opportunity to understand life in a sound and wholesome way."

—Daisy in a speech given in 1924 at Mercer College, Macon, Georgia

Daisy arrived in Cloudlands, Georgia, in 1921, tramping through the wilderness of Lookout Mountain, over big boulders and across rivers. She had been searching for a special spot of natural beauty and peace, a camp where Girl Scout leaders would train, and the girls could swim, hike, explore nature, play games, and tell stories around campfires. Her colleagues Dorris Hough and Frances King had located this spot, and Daisy had come to approve it. Here were ten acres for sale near Little River, as well as a natural swimming hole surrounded by enormous stones. There were numerous natural rock outcroppings, rhododendron patches, and trickling brooks.

Brothers John and Will Ledbetter, who owned the land, said the swimming hole would not be part of the deal, but Daisy thought the girls would love it, and she persisted. In the end she bought it all and named it "Camp Juliette Low." The swimming hole, eight feet deep in the middle and five feet deep around the sides, was christened "The Basin." Hundreds of girls descended upon the camp each summer. Daisy relished telling stories and reading the girls' palms around the campfire. She loved the way being outdoors brought their senses alive and helped them come up with questions about why rivers flowed a certain direction and how rocks formed. Here, the girls' sense of wonder was heightened. Camp Juliette Low is now an independently owned, nonprofit, 330-acre camp for girls who canoe, fish, hike, and have the outdoor adventures Daisy pictured that first day.

Being outside was a beloved part of Daisy's childhood. She would play for hours and hours with her brothers, sisters, and cousins, who would meet in the summer at Etowah Cliffs in Cartersville, Georgia. There, they would not only explore nature, but put on creative plays, complete with costumes.

It is fitting that one of Daisy's final accomplishments—one she fought for as she was in the early stages of terminal breast cancer—brought more girls and leaders together from around the world than any other camp before. It was the Fourth International Conference of Girl Guides and Girl Scouts, held at Camp Edith Macy in Briarcliff, New York, just outside New York City, in 1926. The conference was the first of these international camps to be in a country other than England, and Daisy was the mistress of ceremonies, both behind and in front of the scenes. There were 456 representatives from twenty-nine countries present, all of them dedicated to encouraging leadership in young women. The 269-acre Camp Macy, set beautifully on the Hudson River, was given as a memorial to the Girl Scouts in honor of Edith Carpenter Macy, who was a National Board member from 1919 until 1925. Her husband donated the property and an endowment to the Girl Scouts in honor of his wife after her death in 1925.

B-P and his wife, Olave Baden-Powell, were in attendance, making it more special to Daisy. Everyone had told her that Macy wouldn't be ready that year for the conference, but Daisy pushed ahead, knowing it was that year or never for her. She had missed a big convention in Saint Louis a few months before when she was too sick to travel. The camp, on which construction had begun just the year before, was finished with not a moment to spare, with construction workers being led out the back door as the guests came in the front. Holding the conference in New York after the first three years in England helped contribute to the international feel of Girl Scouting. Future world conferences would be held in Poland, Switzerland, Sweden, Brazil, Singapore, Japan, Iran, and many more nations.

Just after the conference, in a May 1926 letter, Girl Scout National Director Jane Deeter Rippin wrote to Daisy: "I know that everyone who was there got from that meeting inspiration and a truer understanding of the ideals of Scouting. It was a wonderful experience to us all to have the Founder of the Boy Scouts and the Founder of the Girl Scouts of the United States with us together at Camp Edith Macy."

Earlier that year, Daisy had been told (by her friend and physician, Dr. Stuart McGuire) that she had about six months to live. As soon as she received the news, Daisy began dealing with unfinished business. Dr. McGuire and his wife Ruth had already planned a trip to England, so Daisy took the opportunity to travel with them on the same ship. She did not wallow in her illness. One day she told everyone it was her birthday (it was not), and her traveling companions hurried to throw a party with champagne, a beautiful dinner, and a birthday cake with candles, presented by the ship's chef. On the same trip she attended a masquerade ball wearing a sheet, a pillow case on her head, and empty liquor bottles hanging on her by strings. She called herself "Departed Spirits," and was very pleased to report to her friends that she won a prize for her costume. She returned to Savannah just ten days before she died. At the time of her death there were more than 140,000 girls enrolled in Girl Scouts, with 5,250 troops in each state in the country.

Daisy died at her Savannah home in 1927. Most people didn't know she was sick; it was a time when cancer was not talked about openly. Letters and messages poured into the Girl Scout headquarters from troops in California, Ohio, Florida, West Virginia, and scores more. International groups in Hungary, Liberia, Canada, and many others sent heartfelt condolences. People who had never even met Daisy felt they knew her through her work with the Girl Scouts. Daisy had requested that she be buried in her Girl Scout uniform, with the Silver Fish Award and a Thanks Badge made of jewels that B-P had given her in 1919 in front of three thousand girls at Carnegie Hall in New York on behalf of the Girl Scouts. In her uniform pocket was a telegram from the national Girl Scout office reading: "You are not only the first Girl Scout, you are the best Girl Scout of them all."

IN 1924, A UNIFORMED JULIETTE LOW CHATS WITH THE AMERICAN
DELEGATION OF GIRL SCOUTS AT THE GIRL SCOUT AND GIRL GUIDE
WORLD CAMP AT FOXLEASE, ENGLAND.

B-P wrote a memoriam to Daisy honoring her attributes of love, humor, courage, keenness, and common sense. "It is largely thanks to these qualities in that one great-hearted woman that Scouting took its root and gained the widespread power for good it holds today among the girlhood of America," he wrote in a July 1927 letter intended for use in a Girl Scout memorial remembrance book after her death.

Daisy's friend, the author Rudyard Kipling, wrote: "Her own good-angels looked after her even when she was on one wheel over a precipice; and there was nobody like her," in a 1928 letter to Daisy's brother Arthur Gordon.

One of the things many people remembered about Daisy was that from the beginning of the Girl Scouts, she steadfastly promoted camping as one of the truest and best activities for girls. She loved how it took the girls away from their everyday thoughts and brought them into a life of trees and grass and clouds. There was time, when camping, to stare at the sky or skip stones in the river. She also believed camping offered an opportunity to explore and was a key way to build community, as each girl took on a "kaper" or task, from preparing meals to planting trees. She trusted fresh air as a sort of antidote to difficulties and bad health. Cooking was important, both as a necessity and as a way to enjoy food in a communal setting. The Girl Scouts are credited with inventing the first s'mores, those gooey, delicious sandwich concoctions of marshmallow toasted over an open fire, chocolate, and graham cracker. They published what appears to be the first s'mores recipe in 1927, in a book called *Tramping and Trailing with the Girl Scouts.* The story goes that everyone who had one asked for "s'more."

Girl Scouts have long been environmental advocates, from their conservation efforts to their work with wildlife and water. In 2011, more than one thousand Scouts in Pennsylvania launched a "Forever Green" initiative, which focuses on encouraging environmentally sound practices, such as biking, composting, and recycling. One of the group's tenets is to "use resources wisely," and girls have been working toward a better understanding of the "leave no trace" ethic, which encourages people to enjoy the natural environment while making minimal impact on it.

Girl Scout councils around the country now run campsites, and the experience is considered essential for the girls. In Wisconsin, we have Girl Scout camps for horseback riding, interior design, survivor skills, and engineering. I remember what was once the Rockwood Girl Scout National Center near where I grew up in Potomac, Maryland. Rockwood was a house next to a walking trail that my parents and I would hike on regularly, along the C & O Canal, near the Great Falls Lock. It was given to the Girl Scouts in 1936 in the will of Carolyn G. Caughey, who used it as a vacation house until she died. Rockwood, with its "Manor House" and "Carolyn's Cottage," had a heyday in the 1950s, when troop houses were built and many Girl

Scouts came for camping trips on the grounds. But in 1979, Rockwood was sold to the State of Maryland, and it is now used for weddings, conferences, and other events.

After renovation and a re-dedication in 1982, "Macy" (the Edith Macy Conference Center in New York) has become that wilderness retreat for leaders, known since its founding as the "University in the Woods." Camp Andree Clark, right across the street from Camp Macy, was given to the Girl Scouts in 1921 by Montana senator and copper baron William Clark and his wife, in memory of their daughter Andree, a Girl Scout who had died at age sixteen.

Through the decades, the girls have discovered they can't replicate gathering in person, whether they try by telegram, email, or text message, though of all of Daisy's lessons, this is one that unfortunately I can feel and see slipping away. If we don't give our children the opportunities and resources to be outside, they will miss an entire aspect of living. We are aware of this as our family drives through the gorgeous rolling Wisconsin hills and our kids are glued to the car's DVD player, and when a late-summer afternoon at the lake turns into dueling iPhone battles. I spent many years as a technology reporter and have a geeky interest in tech and gadgets too, but it seems unnatural to see kids choosing to play a video game rather than climb a tree.

The good news is the recognition of how nature plays a role in our lives, by Girl Scouts' encouragement of camping and outdoor activities, and by modern philosophers such as Richard Louv, whose book *Last Child in the Woods* delves into what he calls nature-deficit disorder and how we can inspire or reinspire our children. There's a larger purpose here than just creating wild boys and girls. The most successful leaders of the future, Louv says, will be "nature-smart," and better able to navigate the real world as well as the virtual one.

Although she was not a Girl Scout leader, environmental writer Rachel Carson, author of *Silent Spring*, was deeply involved in teaching children about nature and preservation. Originally a marine biologist, her groundbreaking book shed light on problems caused by pesticides in our society. In her book *A Sense of Wonder*, she wrote: "For the child…it is not half so important to know as to feel. If facts are the seeds that later produce knowledge and wisdom, then the emotions and the impressions of the senses are the fertile soil in which the seeds must grow…It is more important to pave the way for a child to want to know than to put him on a diet of facts that he is not ready to assimilate."

Here in Madison, we are fortunate to be neighbors with the Aldo Leopold Nature Center, named for the Wisconsin conservationist and philosopher. This is a place where people of all ages can step out of their city shoes and thoughts, and into a world where the animal noises and the swish of tall grasses perform a daily symphony. The center teaches lessons about tadpoles and frogs, maple syrup harvesting, and wildflowers, among dozens of other nature topics. "That land is a community is the basic concept of ecology, but that land is to be loved and respected is an extension of ethics," Leopold once said.

A close friend of Daisy's for decades, Rudyard Kipling, the Nobel-prize-winning writer, wrote the children's classics *The Jungle Book* and *Kim*. In *The Jungle Book*, a boy named Mowgli becomes part of an animal family and learns to live in the wild. Kipling's wife, Carrie, was a distant relative of Daisy's, and Daisy often spent time with the couple in England. B-P used many of Kipling's names in

The Jungle Book for the Cub Scouts, the younger version of Boy Scouts. "Akela," father of the wolf in *The Jungle Book*, is the name for the Cub Scout master. "Baloo" (the bear) and "Bagheera" (the panther) are the assistant Cubmasters. Kipling and Daisy shared a love of the outdoors and a fascination with the natural world. Daisy would tell a story about the night she and Kipling escaped a fancy party—in full evening dress—to run down to the river and fish for salmon.

A vital benefit of spending increased time outdoors is moving more. Swimming, horseback riding, running, soccer, basketball, all these sports are good for the physical health of the girls. Childhood obesity has become a severe problem in our society. About 17 percent of children and adolescents in the United States are obese, triple the number from one generation ago. A sedentary, indoor lifestyle is taking its toll, and we know it, yet it is getting worse. Overweight kids are more likely to have health issues, including heart disease and type 2 diabetes; social and psychological problems, such as lower self-esteem; and are more likely to become overweight adults (Centers for Disease Control and Prevention, Atlanta, Georgia).

There have been some steps forward. In

2010, Michelle Obama (who, as the First Lady, continues the tradition of serving as Girl Scout Honorary National President) created Let's Move, a campaign against childhood obesity that works with kids to teach lessons on food, exercise, and social issues. Let's Move addresses all sides of the problem, from prenatal care to school lunches, access to playgrounds, and after-school physical activities. There are more great programs, such as Girls on the Run, a nonprofit started in Charlotte, North Carolina, which uses running as a way to empower girls physically and emotionally. At the fun Girls Rock Camp this past summer, my daughter learned electric guitar, jewelry making, and

GIRL SCOUTS CAMP MEAL, CIRCA 1917.

punk-rock aerobics from her musician teachers, who also gave a class in self-esteem. And in Girl Scouts, we make the camping experience—hiking, setting up tents, canoeing, and the rest of the wonderful outdoor activities—part of our tradition of moving and having a good time.

When we begin talking in our troop about our annual "encampment," our overnight camping trip with about one hundred and fifty Madison-area Girl Scouts, the energy in the room creates a real, audible buzz. There are so many parts they love—sleeping in a cabin or tent, putting on a play, making s'mores over the campfire, trading handmade pins, and meeting new friends. As we make lists of gear to pack, assign duties, and create our troop flag for the year, it becomes clear that camping, like so many other parts of life—school, work, exercise—is not just about one thing, but a multitude of experiences. Our area has been doing the encampment for more than twenty-five years now, but every year is a bit different.

Our first year of encampment, we had eleven girls and nine moms sleep overnight—a pretty good ratio. I have to admit I was worried ahead of time about the then seven-year-olds missing their parents or not being able to sleep. I shouldn't

OUR TROOP'S PACKING LIST
FOR OVERNIGHT ENCAMPMENT

* First aid kit
* Water bottle (best to have one that can have hot and cold and can attach with a clip to a belt)
* SWAPS
* Hand sanitizer
* Pillow
* Sleeping bag
* Camping mat
* Tent (if not in a cabin)
* Binoculars
* Picnic blanket
* Rain boots
* Raincoat
* Two sets of clothes
* Extra socks and shoes
* Toothbrush and toothpaste
* Hairbrush, hairbands
* Flashlight
* Plastic bags for projects, garbage, wet clothes
* Sun hat
* Warm hat and gloves
* Uniform sash or vest
* Sunblock
* Sit-upons
* Notebook and pencils

have—they were independent, excited, and had an absolute blast. It did help to warn them ahead of time about the pit toilets—no flushing available. From the beginning, as we rode out to the Madison School Forest, a wonderful nearby campground, they sang songs, and it was clear they were in it together.

As one of the youngest groups, we were assigned a nice roomy cabin, nothing fancy (not even bunk beds), but we had a roof over our heads and room enough to lay out our sleeping bags in straight lines and listen to a group bedtime story. The problem was the cabin doubled as the nature center—so it was fully equipped with taxidermy of all sorts—real stuffed birds, raccoons, and small cats. We had heard there would be exhibits, but hadn't really pictured these. The kids joked about it at first, but as it got darker, some of them started talking about the dead animals. The dead animals were all around. We covered the animals as best we could and moved on to storytelling with flashlights turned off. Thankfully the girls were so exhausted from the fun day that they soon forgot about the animals and drifted off to sleep.

Girl Scouts love their traditions. One of our girls' favorites at camping or other big gatherings is SWAPS, which stands for Special Whatchmacallits Affectionately Pinned Somewhere. The first swapping can be traced back to the 1950s or 1960s, and it has now become a treasured activity. Each troop chooses a design of their own and creates (usually one hundred or more) small, swappable, pinnable keepsakes. This past year we did mini-clipboards, simply small pieces of paper clipped with a binder clip on a piece of wood. They slipped a safety pin on the handle part of the binder clip, and wrote their troop number on the back. They loved them. Each girl then gets a small bag full of her troop's SWAPS (so if there are ten girls, each gets ten) to trade. It's very sweet to see scores of young girls holding their SWAPS, making their way through the crowd, bartering at first shyly and then with great excitement. It's both icebreaker and treasure-hunt. Then, back in the cabin or tent, the girls spill out their SWAPS, comparing and trading some more, and pinning them on their sashes or vests. We make a banner ahead of time too, a big felt poster that all the girls work on independently (creating a special piece) and together.

Encampment is also our time for the beloved bridging ceremonies. This is when girls "bridge" from one level of Girl Scout to the next, from Girl Scout Daisies to Girl Scout Brownies, then Girl Scout Juniors,

WHAT'S IN OUR TROOP'S FIRST AID KIT

* Adhesive tape
* Alcohol wipes
* Bandages
* Drinking cup
* Flashlight
* Gauze pads
* Instant ice pack
* List of emergency telephone numbers
* Matches
* Needle
* Safety pins
* Scissors
* Splints
* Thermometer
* Tweezers

Girl Scout Cadettes, Girl Scout Seniors, and Girl Scout Ambassadors. In our troop, girls stand on one side of a little wooden bridge, walk over it, and are handed their new uniform, or a hat, pin, or token, on the other side by an older sister (sometimes they're matched with their birth sister, but usually it's their Girl Scout sister). In different parts of the country, all kinds of bridges are used. Some San Francisco Girl Scouts have bridged by walking over the Golden Gate Bridge, a beautiful backdrop for their day.

The symbolism of bridging is powerful, and I can't overstate how much they love it. They're moving up in the world in their own ways, getting older, and knowing more about themselves and the world around them. The big kids remember when they were the littlest Girl Scouts, and the smallest girls watch and think about how that will be them, someday.

Back at the Girl Scout National Historic Preservation Center located at Girl Scout National Headquarters (or "HQ," as they call it) in New York, I had gradually been sifting through historical files in their archives. Pamela Cruz, the friendly and busy (tours, convention planning, and a lot of other things go on there every day) director of the Girl Scout National Historic Preservation Center, wheeled out archival boxes and boxes on metal three-level carts. There I would read letters and documents as I sat by the window, enjoying the view of the city's skyscrapers. I had to wear white gloves since the paper was fragile, and I could use only pencils to take my notes—no pens allowed. Every time I walked through the big glass doors at the HQ entrance, I had to stop for just a few moments to look at the large portrait hanging on the wall of Daisy in her late twenties, just after she was married. It is an image many people have in their minds of her— the one at HQ is a reproduction of the original, which hangs in the National Portrait Gallery in Washington, DC. In it, Daisy is wearing a frothy gown with a full bustle and holding a small fan. Her hair is gently pulled back. Her smile is not quite a smile, but enigmatic, *Mona Lisa*-like. She is beautiful in this portrait, but her eyes are wistful. As I sat back down to research, I always wondered what she was thinking at the time that painting was made.

Many of the files were organized by year, and as I got closer to 1927, the year of Daisy's death, her writing became shakier, and she started to write about being sick. It would have been difficult for the recipients of her letters to know how ill Daisy really was. They would get clues when she said she had to skip a big Girl Scout event she would have otherwise never missed, but the details of her struggle with cancer were not there.

As Daisy slowed down, so did my reading. I knew how this story was going to end, and how close this ending was. Waiting for me in the final files were scores of condolence letters. I had been on such a journey finding out about Daisy and was having so much fun. More importantly, there was more she could have done, as the Girl Scouts had been about to enter a huge growth period. I got up and took a break and came back later, because I didn't want it to be over. I didn't want her to die.

But then I realized I'm still learning, still on the path she started, each time Melissa and Sherry and I are with our troop, every time we "shake out the sillies" or encourage the girls to earn a badge. Daisy's influence is far

Juliette Gordon Low, "Daisy," is buried in the Laurel Grove Cemetery in Savannah, Ga. Her headstone reads, from 1 Corinthians 13:13:

Now abideth faith, hope and love, but the greatest of these is love.

from over, for so many of us, and will continue, even years after our troop has grown up, with each new Girl Scout "Daisy" sister.

timeline

October 31, 1860—Juliette Magill Kinzie Gordon, nicknamed "Daisy," is born in Savannah, Georgia.

1865—The Civil War ends with the North defeating the South.

1865—Daisy goes to school with Mme. Lucille Blois, Savannah, Georgia.

1873–1874—Daisy attends Miss Emmet's School, Morristown, New Jersey.

1874–1875—Daisy goes to Virginia Female Institute boarding school in Staunton, Virginia (now Stuart Hall School).

1877–1878—Daisy attends Edge Hill Boarding School in Keswick Station, Virginia.

1878–1879—Daisy moves to Mesdemoiselles Charbonniers, a French finishing school in New York City.

1882—Daisy goes on her first trip abroad to Europe.

1885—Daisy loses partial hearing in one ear after a botched treatment for an earache.

1886—Daisy marries William Mackay Low, "Billow," in Savannah, Georgia.

1886—At their wedding, a grain of rice lodges in Daisy's other ear and eventually causes her to lose hearing in that ear.

1887—Daisy and Billow move to England.

1905—Billow dies before the couple finalizes their divorce.

1911—Daisy meets Sir Robert Baden-Powell, "B-P," founder of the Boy Scouts.

1912—Daisy gathers the first American Girl Scouts for a meeting in Savannah, Georgia.

1915—Daisy is named as the first president of the Girl Scouts of America.

1926—Daisy leads the Fourth International Conference of Girl Guides and Girl Scouts at Camp Edith Macy in New York.

1927—On January 17, in Savannah, Daisy dies from breast cancer at age sixty-six.

1948—A United States postage stamp featuring Daisy's picture is issued.

1953—The Girl Scouts buy and restore Daisy's Savannah childhood home, known as the Juliette Gordon Low Girl Scout National Center, or "The Birthplace."

1979—Daisy is inducted into the National Women's Hall of Fame in Seneca Falls, New York.

2005—Daisy is honored by a medallion on a Washington, DC, sidewalk near the White House called "The Extra Mile Points of Light Volunteer Pathway."

2012—Girl Scouts of the USA celebrates one hundred years since its founding by Juliette Gordon Low, "Daisy."

daisy's circle of family and friends

* Juliette Magill Gordon Low—"Daisy," founder of the Girl Scouts of the USA (1860–1927)

* William Washington Gordon II—Daisy's father; a Savannah cotton broker, Yale graduate, and Confederate officer who rose to the ranks of Brigadier General in the United States Volunteer Army during the Spanish-American War

* Eleanor (Nellie) Kinzie Gordon—Daisy's mother; originally from Chicago, had six children (Daisy was the second), and was remembered as the "Angel of the Boys in Blue" for setting up a hospital for soldiers in Miami returning from the Spanish-American War

* William Washington Gordon I—Daisy's paternal grandfather; founder of the Central of Georgia Railroad, Mayor of Savannah 1834–1836, first person from Georgia to graduate from the United States Military Academy at West Point

* Sarah Anderson Stites Gordon—Daisy's paternal grandmother; niece of Supreme Court Justice James Moore Wayne

* John Harris Kinzie—Daisy's maternal grandfather; one of the first settlers of Chicago, expert in tribal Indian languages, Indian Agent to the Winnebago Tribe in Wisconsin

* Juliette Augusta Magill Kinzie—Daisy's maternal grandmother

* William Mackay Low—"Billow," Daisy's husband, whom she married in 1886

* Andrew Low—Billow's father; a cotton broker with interests in Savannah and England

* Mary Cowper Stiles Low—Billow's mother

* Eleanor Gordon—Daisy's oldest sister, Nellie

* Sarah Alice Gordon—Daisy's younger sister, Alice

* W. W. Gordon III—Daisy's younger brother, Willie

* Mabel Gordon—Daisy's youngest sister

* George Arthur Gordon—Daisy's youngest brother

* Margaret Gordon Lawrence—The namesake niece of Daisy Low; called "Daisy Doots" by her family, first registered Girl Scout in the United States

* Nina Anderson Pape—Daisy's cousin who received the telephone call, "Come right over…"

* Sir Robert Baden-Powell ("B-P")—Founder of the Boy Scouts of America; friend of Daisy's

* Agnes Baden-Powell—Sister of B-P; helped launch the British Girl Guides

* Olave Baden-Powell—Wife of B-P and Chief Guide, 1918, Scout and Guide leader

* Rudyard Kipling—Celebrated author; friend of Daisy's

* Jane Deeter Rippin—Girl Scout National Director 1919–1930

* Ann Hyde Clarke Choate—Second President of the Girl Scouts 1920–1922; one of the founders of the Juliette Low World Friendship Fund, Daisy's goddaughter

* Sarah Louise Arnold—National Director 1925–1926; first dean of Simmons College 1901–1919

* Lou Henry Hoover—National Director 1922–1925 and 1935–1937; Honorary President (as First Lady) 1929–1933

* Helen Osborne Storrow—First Vice President of the Girl Scouts 1920–1922; donated Our Chalet in Switzerland to the World Association

* Edith Carpenter Macy—Chairman of the Board 1919–1925; Camp Edith Macy in New York is named after her and dedicated to her by her husband after her death

bibliography and further reading

Most of the historical information used in *On My Honor* came from original letters, documents, and notes, as well as the personal guidance of the archivists at:

- The Girl Scouts of the USA National Historic Preservation Center, New York, NY
- Juliette Gordon Low Birthplace, Savannah, GA
- Georgia Historical Society, Savannah, GA

The following books and websites were helpful in my research or might be interesting for more information.

BOOKS

Arnold, Sarah Louise. *The Way of Understanding.* New York: Girl Scouts of the USA, 1934.

Carson, Rachel. *Silent Spring.* New York: Houghton Mifflin, 1962.

———. *The Sense of Wonder.* New York: Harper Collins, 1965.

Daiss, Timothy. *Rebels, Saints and Sinners: Savannah's Rich History and Colorful Personalities.* Gretna: Pelican Publishing Co., 2002.

Degenhardt, Mary and Kirsch, Judith. *Girl Scout Collector's Guide: A History of Uniforms, Insignia, Publications, and Memorabilia.* Lubbock: Texas University Press, 2005.

Jones, Jacqueline. *Saving Savannah: The City and the Civil War.* New York: Vintage Books, 2009.

Isaacson, Rupert. *The Horse Boy: A Memoir of Healing.* New York: Back Bay Books, 2009.

Kinzie, Juliette Augusta. *Wau-Bun: The Early Day in the Northwest.* Carlisle: Applewood Books, originally published in 1856.

Lindbergh, Anne Morrow. *Gift from the Sea.* New York: Pantheon, 1955, 1975.

Louv, Richard. *Last Child in the Woods.* Chapel Hill: Algonquin Books, 2005, 2008.

McConnell, Patricia. *For the Love of a Dog.* New York: Ballantine, 2007.

Pipher, Mary, PhD. *Reviving Ophelia: Saving the Selves of Adolescent Girls.* New York: Riverhead Books, 1994.

Proctor, Tammy M. *Scouting for Girls.* Santa Barbara: Praeger, an imprint of ABC-CLIO, 2009.

Shore, Bill. *The Cathedral Within: Transforming Your Life by Giving Something Back.* New York: Random House, 1999.

Shultz, Gladys Denny and Lawrence, Daisy Gordon.

Lady from Savannah: The Life of Juliette Gordon Low. New York: Girl Scouts of the USA, 1958.

Simmons, Rachel. *Odd Girl Out: The Hidden Culture of Aggression in Girls.* New York: Harcourt Inc., 2002.

———. *The Curse of the Good Girl: Raising Authentic Girls with Courage and Confidence.* New York: The Penguin Press, 2009.

Vetter, Marjorie, ed. *Stories to Live By: A Treasury of Fiction from The American Girl.* New York: The Platt & Munk Co., Inc., 1960.

Wiseman, Rosalind. *Queen Bees and Wannabes: Helping Your Daughter Survive Cliques, Gossip, Boyfriends, and the New Realities of Girl World.* New York: Three Rivers Press, 2002.

WEBSITES

The Andrew Low House: www.andrewlowhouse.com

First Headquarters (Girl Scouts of Savannah, GA): www.gshg.org/

The Girl Scouts of the USA official site: www.girlscouts.org/

The Juliette Gordon Low Birthplace: www.juliettegordonlowbirthplace.org/

The Juliette Low World Friendship Fund: www.girlscouts.org/who_we_are/global/juliette_low_fund.asp

The World Association of Girl Guides and Girl
   Scouts: www.wagggsworld.org/en/home

notes

v   *Have you ever stopped to think*: <u>How Girls Can Help Their Country</u>, adapted from Agnes Baden-Powell and Sir Robert Baden-Powell's Handbook (1916).

4   *Girl Scouts are currently*: "Public Policy and Advocacy," http://www.girlscouts.org/who_we_are/advocacy/.

6   *It is what we need now*: "Facts," http://www.girlscouts.org/who_we_are/facts/.

12   *Daisy instructed the recipient*: letter from Daisy to "Dearest Jane," January 10, 1933.

CHAPTER ONE

21   *Scouting rises within you*: <u>The Rally</u> magazine, January 1919.

27   *According to a remembrance called*: "Juliette Gordon Low Grown-Up," by Daisy Gordon Lawrence, remembrance, Georgia Historical Society.

28   *I learn new things*: "Juliette Gordon Low Grown-Up," by Daisy Gordon Lawrence, remembrance, Georgia Historical Society, Savannah, Georgia.

28   *In an 1871 letter*: Letter from Daisy's mother, Eleanor (Nellie) Kinzie Gordon, to Daisy, 1871, Georgia Historical Society.

29   *Daisy's brother Arthur described*: "Juliette Low as Her Family Knew Her," by G. Arthur Gordon, remembrance, Georgia Historical Society.

30   *In January 1877*: Letter from Daisy to her mother, January 1877, Georgia Historical Society.

30   *Her mind did not:* "Juliette Low as Her Family Knew Her," by G. Arthur Gordon, remembrance, Georgia Historical Society.

30   *But, Mama, I can't keep:* Letter from Daisy to her mother, January 1877, Georgia Historical Society.

CHAPTER TWO

38   *From then on:* "When I was a Girl," by Juliette Gordon Low, *The American Girl* magazine, October 1926.

39   *Their efforts were lauded:* <u>Good Angel of the Boys in Blue: Eleanor Kinzie Gordon's Wartime Summer, 1898</u>, by Jacqueline E. Clancy. Georgia Southern Press, 2002.

CHAPTER THREE

49   *Girl Scouts learn that being kind:* <u>How Girls Can Help Their Country</u>, page 273, 1933.

51   *One day, when Daisy:* "Juliette Low's School Days," by Daisy Gordon Lawrence, Georgia Historical Society.

51   *When Daisy was a little girl:* "My Aunt Daisy was the First Girl Scout," by Arthur Gordon, Woman's Day, March 1956.

51   *At one point…to be fed with the animals:* "Juliette Low as her Family Knew Her," by G. Arthur Gordon, remembrance, Georgia Historical Society.

52   *One Thanksgiving:* "My Aunt Daisy was the First Girl Scout," by Arthur Gordon, *Woman's Day*, March 1956.

53   *Over the years:* "Juliette Low as her Family Knew Her," by G. Arthur Gordon, remembrance, Georgia Historical Society.

CHAPTER FOUR

61   *Health is probably:* <u>Scouting for Girls, the Official Handbook of the Girl Scouts</u>, 1920.

65   *Daisy brought her cook:* "Centennial Receipt Book: Juliette Gordon Low Hostess and Homemaker 1860–1960" Girl Scouts of the USA, 1960.

67   *"I think Mrs. Bateman…":* Letter from Daisy to her father, William Washington Gordon II, January 1902, Georgia Historical Society.

68   *Daisy wrote a poem called*: "The Creative Arts of Juliette Gordon Low," Robertine K. McClendon, 1960.

70   *Scouting is the cradle*: "The History and Activities of Girl Scouts," by Juliette Gordon Low, (undated).

71   *Daisy wrote in an undated document*: "The History and Activities of Girl Scouts," by Juliette Gordon Low (undated).

79   *The First Girl Scout Cookie Recipe*: <u>The American Girl</u> magazine, July 1922.

CHAPTER FIVE

85   *Badges mean*: 1924 speech by Daisy at Mercer College, Macon, Georgia, Georgia Historical Society.

89   *I looked into the lines*: Daisy's diary, May 30, 1911, Juliette Gordon Low Birthplace, Savannah, Georgia.

89   *Today in the few moments*: Daisy's diary, June 1, 1911, Juliette Gordon Low Birthplace.

90   *There are little stars*: Daisy's diary, June 17, 1911, Juliette Gordon Low Birthplace.

CHAPTER SIX

97   *Truly ours is a circle of*: Halloween letter written by Juliette Gordon Low, 1925.

101   *In an October 1916 letter*: Letter from Daisy to Mabel, 1916, Georgia Historical Society.

103   *In May 1912*: Letter from Daisy to her parents, May 1912, Juliette Gordon Low, Georgia Historical Society.

104   *Both girls had to row*: Letter from Daisy to her parents, May 1912, Juliette Gordon Low Birthplace Savannah, Georgia.

104   *She wrote home…I like girls*: Letter from Daisy to her father, August 1911, Georgia Historical Society.

105   *My happy, happy year*: "Juliette Gordon School Days," remembrance by Daisy Gordon Lawrence, Georgia Historical Society.

CHAPTER SEVEN

CHAPTER EIGHT

133   *Girl Scouting is not just knowing*: The Girl Scout Handbook, by Walter John Hoxie, 1956.

137   *Hoxie particularly excelled…A tree is a tree*: How Girls Can Help Their Country, adapted from Agnes Baden-Powell and Sir Robert Baden-Powell's Handbook, 1916.

137   *There is much…As it may happen*: adapted from Agnes Baden-Powell and Sir Robert Baden-Powell's Handbook, 1916.

138   *It is the aim*: "Informational Pamphlet," Girl Scouts Incorporated, President Juliette Gordon Low (undated).

140   *But in addition…Have you ever stopped* (and other quotes in this section): adapted from Agnes Baden-Powell and Sir Robert Baden-Powell's Handbook, 1916.

142   *The advice is…Any bad smell*: How Girls Can Help Their Country, p. 97, adapted from Agnes Baden-Powell and Sir Robert Baden-Powell's Handbook, 1916.

142   *Recipe ideas…Boiling water is useful*: How Girls Can Help Their Country, p. 112, adapted from Agnes Baden-Powell and Sir Robert Baden-Powell's Handbook, 1916.

142   *Girls were assured that…Needlework*: How Girls Can Help Their Country, p. 107, adapted from Agnes Baden-Powell and Sir Robert Baden-Powell's Handbook, 1916.

143   *As it says in an early*: How Girls Can Help Their Country, p. 58, adapted from Agnes Baden-Powell and Sir Robert Baden-Powell's Handbook, 1916.

144   *Each one of us*: adapted from Agnes Baden-Powell and Sir Robert Baden-Powell's Handbook, 1916.

CHAPTER NINE

151   *I hope that we shall all*: Halloween birthday message, Juliette Gordon Low, 1924.

155   *One of her young friends…She had a wicked wit*: Lady from Savannah: The Life of Juliette Gordon Low, by Daisy Gordon Lawrence and Gladys Denny Schulz, 1958.

acknowledgments

First, thank you, Daisy. You created something that not only lasts, but renews through each generation and affects millions of girls. That is a rare accomplishment, especially for a woman who thought her life was over before she even heard of the Girl Scouts.

The Girl Scouts of the USA were wonderfully supportive in my writing of this book. Fran Powell Harold, Director, and Katherine Keena, Program Manager, of the Juliette Gordon Low Birthplace in Savannah welcomed me to their beautiful city, where I was able to walk through Daisy's homes and see firsthand the iron gates she forged, her sculptures, and her intricately painted china. Fran and Katherine are the true "JGL Mavens" and have guided me in the right direction many times.

Nora Lewis, Director of the Library and Archives at the Georgia Historical Society in Savannah, helped me delve through hundreds of letters written by and to Daisy, her parents, friends, and relatives. At the Girl Scout Headquarters in New

York, Director of the Girl Scout National Historic Preservation Center Pamela Cruz, and archivist Yevgeniya Gribov, set me up with a research spot next to their archives, where I was able to read more original letters, diaries, and stories. Pamela helped me look through archival photographs of Daisy for this book. Jami Brantley at the First Headquarters—Daisy's carriage house that held the early Girl Scout meetings in Savannah—welcomed me with a candle to light, signifying the passing of the Girl Scout flame, in their little courtyard. Thanks to my home Girl Scout Badgerland Council, especially our council CEO Marci Henderson, for supporting our troop. Most of the research for this book came from primary sources such as letters and documents, as well as my own experiences as a Girl Scout troop leader.

My agents, Jan Miller and Nena Madonia (a former Girl Scout herself) at Dupree Miller & Associates, were enthusiastic from the start about this book and are great allies to have in your corner. Thank you to publisher Dominique Raccah and editors Peter Lynch and Kelly Bale at Sourcebooks for their excitement and work on the book.

Thanks to my co-troop leaders and good friends, Melissa Auchard Scholz and Sherry

Huhn Gotzler, for reading the manuscript and for their humor and passion for this great volunteer job we do. I am lucky to get to work and play with them.

I often say I learn the most from the girls, and I want to give a huge hug and thank you to each and every one in our troop. You are all such cool girls. Thanks also to their parents for this experience. The dads are great too, but I want to particularly single out the moms for their support and friendship, as I have talked to many of them about various parts of this book: Martha Alibali, Alison Alter, Shawn Doherty, Calliope Jordahl, Valerie LaLuzerne, Karolyn Pionek, Dana Scheckel, Renee Thomas, and Pam Wittenwyler, and to our newest mom Lilly Lukindo.

Thanks to my wonderful women friends who are my sisters all over the country, especially Alison Bermack, Evelyn Wilder, Suzanne Swift, Alison Meyer, Gail Mandel, Janina Wetzel, and Daniela Deane, who encouraged me in many ways while writing this book. Thanks to my neighborhood book club women (big girls still need to hang out), who keep me reading, discussing, thinking big thoughts, and drinking good wine: Lainie Barber, Jennifer Collins, Erica Fox Gehrig, Emily Hall,

Marnie Hulan, Julia Kerr, Annie Levihn, Beth Rogers, Kristin Shadman, Renee Thomas, Emily Whelan, and Haley Weygandt.

My parents, Patrick and Dee Henry, are always a great source of inspiration and encouragement and I am so grateful for them. Thanks to all the members of my family, especially George Kleiber and Diane Dabich, Beverly and Ron Raphael, Lesley and Dave Kitts, and my niece, Samantha Kitts.

My daughters, Eve and Julia, both Girl Scouts, have grown to know Daisy as I've been researching and writing, and I want to thank them for asking great questions and for their patience when they thought I should have finished already. They are why I have written this book and why it ultimately matters. Finally, thanks and love to my husband Ben Kleiber, who, as both critic and fan, is a most valuable reader and person in my life.

about the author

Shannon Henry Kleiber is the author of *The Dinner Club: How the Masters of the Internet Universe Rode the Rise and Fall of the Greatest Boom in History* (Free Press/Simon & Schuster, 2002), and a former staff writer and columnist for the *Washington Post.* She has also written for the *Christian Science Monitor, Washington Technology, American Banker,* and *Edible Madison.*

Shannon lives in Madison, Wisconsin, with her husband and two daughters, where she is a Girl Scout leader of her older daughter's troop. For more information, visit www.shannonhenrykleiber.com.

A portion of the proceeds of this book will be donated to the Girl Scouts of the USA.

31192021325053